D0811622

LOUIS ARMSTRONG

THE OFFSTAGE STORY OF SATCHMO

MICHAEL COGSWELL

PORTLAND, OREGON

Book Design: Wade Daughtry, Collectors Press, Inc.

Library of Congress Cataloging-in-Publication Data
Cogswell, Michael.
  Louis Armstrong : the offstage story of Satchmo / Michael Cogswell.--
1st American ed.
     p. cm.
Includes bibliographical references (p.   ) and index.
  ISBN 1-888054-81-6 (hardcover : alk. paper)
  1. Armstrong, Louis, 1901-1971--Sources. 2. Louis Armstrong House and
Archives. 3. Jazz musicians--United States--Biography. I. Title.
  ML419.A75C63 2003
  781.65'092--dc21

                                        2003010166
Printed in Singapore

9 8 7 6 5 4 3 2 1

Collectors Press books are available at special discounts for bulk purchases, premiums, and promotions. Special editions, including personalized inserts or covers, and corporate logos, can be printed in quantity for special purposes. For further information contact: Special Sales, Collectors Press, Inc., P.O. Box 230986 Portland, OR 97281. Toll free: 1-800-423-1848.

For a free catalog write:
Collectors Press, Inc.
P.O. Box 230986
Portland, OR 97281
Toll free: 1-800-423-1848
www.collectorspress.com

To contact the Louis Armstrong
House & Archives:
Louis Armstrong House & Archives
Queens College
Flushing, NY 11367
718-997-3670
www.satchmo.net

All royalties from Louis Armstrong: The Offstage Story of Satchmo support the programs and services of the Louis Armstrong House & Archives at Queens College, New York.

Contents

Louis warming up,
cigarette in hand.

Foreword

About fifteen or sixteen years ago, Howard Brofsky, then a music professor at Queens College (and a pretty good jazz trumpeter), called to ask if I would come to the house of Louis Armstrong and take a look at its contents — the Armstrong "nachlass," so to speak. The college had been selected by the Louis Armstrong Educational Foundation to take charge of these precious materials and I was among the several Armstrong "experts" whose advice was being sought. I said yes before Howard had finished explaining.

It was the strangest feeling to enter the house once again. I knew exactly when I had been there last: on December 18, 1970, with my friend Charlie Graham, because Louis taped a birthday greeting to Ira Gitler, whose party was our next stop. Tyree Glenn was visiting, and our host was in a good mood (even if he hadn't been he would have made believe — Louis Armstrong had the finest manners of anyone I've known). As always after a visit with Pops, I left with my head in the clouds. (I would see him again, but not at home.)

Now there were familiar things, such as that inimitable bathroom, but even from the outside the house seemed changed. In her widowhood, Lucille had, to a large extent, remade things to her liking. The most startling change was that Louis' den, the one room in the house that truly bore his stamp, had vanished — replaced by a perfectly nice but nondescript sitting area.

But what I was there for was to look through Louis' stuff, and that, thankfully, seemed intact. Here were the tapes, in their decorated boxes, and the scrapbooks, which I became so engrossed in that Howard got fidgety. And the records--ranging from vintage operatic 78s to all kinds of LPs, and including acetates from TV and radio shows, and then, to my absolute delight, 12-inch 78 transcriptions from the legendary 1937 Fleishman's Yeast radio programs, not previously known to exist. "Whatever else you do," I told Howard, "make sure that these are kept safe until they can be properly transferred to tape." That was a major discovery, but it was more than clear that Louis' "stuff" was a precious and invaluable legacy worthy of the most dedicated and loving care.

And that is exactly what it got when the folks at Queens College had the good fortune and good sense to find and hire Michael Cogswell, who turned out to be the ideal man for the job of taking charge of (or more precisely, creating) the Louis Armstrong Archives, and then adding the Armstrong House to his responsibilities.

On his first day at Queens, Michael found himself alone in a room at the college's fine new Rosenthal Library with 72 large cartons. He had no assistant and had to forage for a pencil and some paper. That was in 1991. What has been accomplished since then is truly remarkable. The Armstrong Archives could serve as a model for proper processing of a multi-faceted collection, as well-organized and user-friendly as any I've seen. It has presented, at this writing, a unique series of exhibits, each of which has illuminated a particular facet of Louis Armstrong's incredible life and career. It has already, before the formal opening, made the Armstrong House a beloved venue for commemoration of his legacy, with events involving the participation of many great musicians and members of the surrounding community, including the children Louis loved so well. And, glory be, the house has been meticulously restored to what it was when Louis lived there. Even the den has been reincarnated, as close to the original as humanly possible. In these pages, Michael Cogswell will tell you, with great insight and affection, what Louis did there. Indeed, with insight and love, he has given the reader a wonderful annotated tour of what he calls the Offstage Story of Satchmo.

Like Michael's work on the archives and house, this book is a labor of love. As he explains, Michael never met Louis Armstrong — but I think he knows him as well or better than some who did. Surrounded for years by the spirit of Satchmo, Michael has truly become a guardian of the legacy of that immortal genius and warm and generous man. Pops would say, well done! I can hear him say it...

DAN MORGENSTERN
Director
Institute of Jazz Studies
Rutgers University

Introduction

During my twelve years at the Louis Armstrong House & Archives, during which it has been my privilege to catalog Louis's vast personal collection of memorabilia, to assist researchers with using the collections, to administer the project to open his house as a museum, and to make presentations on Louis all over the world, many people have asked me, "When are you going to write a book?" This is that book.

Louis Armstrong was a delightfully eccentric pack rat who lived in the same house for three decades. His beautifully furnished home — now a national historic landmark and a New York City landmark — is a museum and his immense treasure trove of home-recorded tapes, autobiographical manuscripts, collages, scrapbooks, gold records, photographs, snapshots, original music, personal papers, and gold-plated trumpets is preserved at the Louis Armstrong Archives on the campus of Queens College. *Louis Armstrong: The Offstage Story of Satchmo* is the official guide to the Louis Armstrong House & Archives. It includes a wealth of material that is published here for the first time.

WHAT THIS BOOK IS AND WHAT IT IS NOT

Surprisingly, no one has yet written a definitive, multi-volume, narrative biography of Louis Armstrong.[1] And *Louis Armstrong: The Offstage Story of Satchmo* is not intended to be that much-longed for, definitive biography. But it is hoped that this book that will occupy an exceptional place in Armstrong literature and be a delight to Armstrong fans everywhere.

This book contains more than two hundred and fifty images that have never before been published, as well as some of the curatorial staff's favorite images that have been provided to researchers at the Archives. Curiously, although the Louis Armstrong Archives has quickly become the first place to which record companies, magazines, television producers, and others come for information about Louis, and images from our collections have appeared in compact disc booklets, PBS documentaries, jazz history books, academic journals, and magazine ads, our collections are still overwhelmingly untapped. Professional photo researchers — especially ones from magazines or record companies who "need it yesterday" — often ask for photos that they already know. ("Do you guys have that photo of Louis Armstrong playing his trumpet that's on page 10 of the such-and-such book?") Jazz histories and academic journals typically need only one or two photos. And most of our photo requests are for images of Louis in performance — few researchers have explored Louis's life in the dressing room, on the band bus, in the hotel, and at home.

I have intentionally avoided presenting in this book materials that are not held by the Louis Armstrong House & Archives. (Think of me as sort of an Armstrong-obsessed Nero Wolfe.) And I have also avoided using materials that — although held by the Armstrong Archives — have been published again and again. *Louis Armstrong: The Offstage Story of Satchmo* is therefore a catalog of what I believe to be the most intriguing and revealing items in our collections.

INTERPRETING LOUIS

Louis was a prolific diarist who in his lifetime wrote two published autobiographies, more than a dozen magazine articles, and thousands of chatty, informative letters. That Louis created such an output, while engaged in his legendary musical career, is just one hallmark of his genius.

TOP Singing a tune with the big band as Luis Russell looks on approvingly. Band members include Lawrence Lucie (guitar) and Big Sid Catlett (drums). (St. Louis, 1941)

LEFT Discovered in the Louis Armstrong House were more than two hundred leaves of unpublished autobiographical writings. Louis wrote this manuscript, which he titled "Barbershops," very late in his life.

OPPOSITE PAGE Louis adored his fans and they responded in kind.

Discovered in the Armstrong Archives were more than two hundred
leaves of unpublished autobiographical manuscript, and I have
quoted from them at various places
in this book. But Louis — who
never finished the fifth grade —
had a wonderfully idiosyncratic literary style. His prose is delightfully musical, and he clearly uses
punctuation and capitalization in
non-traditional ways to provide
rhythmic emphasis. (Read some
passages out loud and you'll hear
exactly what I mean.) He uses
ellipses as musical rests rather
than as indications of omission. I
have reproduced his punctuation
and capitalization as accurately as
possible and have altered them
only when not doing so would con-
fuse the reader.[2] I have corrected
several obvious misspellings but
have retained misspellings that
seem to have an intentional pho-
netic charm (e.g., Louis writing
"warmpth" instead of "warmth").

Louis appreciated a dirty joke, well
told. And while hanging out with
his buddies backstage or in the
dressing room, he sometimes used
language that would make a sailor

TOP This candid snapshot captures a more serious side of Louis
that he didn't always show to the public. Note the partially opened
tin of Louis Armstrong Lip Salve on the dressing room table. (1960s)

MIDDLE An Extremely rare photo of Louis as "Bottom" in *Swinging
the Dream*, an all black adaptation of Shakespeare's *A Mid-Summer
Nights Dream*. Jackie "Moms" Mabley is at left. (November 1939)

RIGHT Greeting old friends at the Beige Room in Chicago.
Left to right: Dizzy Gillespie, unidentified, Louis, Arvell Shaw,
Big Sid Catlett. (1940s)

blush. To my knowledge, Louis never used profanity in front of children or strangers, or during radio or television broadcasts, or in other inappropriate situations. (However he was not above adroitly slipping one by — while appearing live on the Tommy Dorsey television show, he announced that the tempo of the next number would be, "Not too slow, not too fast, just half-fast.") Included in *Louis Armstrong: The Offstage Story of Satchmo* are transcriptions of candid conversations, personal letters, and autobiographical writings that contain language that some may deem offensive. It is not my intent to offend anyone. I merely prefer to present Louis as he is rather than to censor him.

I am sometimes introduced as "the foremost expert on Louis Armstrong," an appellation that always embarrasses me. There are plenty of people out there who played in Louis's band, lived in Louis's neighborhood, worked with Louis in the recording studio, hung out with him backstage, or shared meals with him after the gig. (Sadly, each year fewer and fewer of these people are still with us.) I never met Louis. When Louis Armstrong passed away in 1971, I had just graduated from high school and was making my first gigs as a professional saxophonist. But as I preserved and cataloged the materials discovered in Louis's house and met people who did know Louis and listened to and read everything I could get my hands on, I began to meet Louis in a singular way. It's been more than twelve years since I first began to work with Louis Armstrong's stuff, and I am more in love with him than ever. I hope that this book will allow you to become as enamored of Louis as I am.

[1] For a richly insightful biography, I highly recommend Gary Giddins's *Satchmo* (New York: Doubleday, 1988).Our web site www.satchmo.net, has additional recommendations of books and recordings.

[2] Several manuscripts from the Louis Armstrong Archives were eventually published in *Louis Armstrong: In His Own Words,* ed. Thomas Brothers, New York: Oxford University Press, 1999. Dr. Brothers faced the same challenge that I did, and I am indebted to him for his example.

RIGHT The pigeon toed stance and dangling trumpet contribute to the relaxation and charm inherent in this portrait. (London, c. 1932)

Louis's Life and Music

THE ALL STARS perform in the film *Goodyear Jazz Concert,* one in a series of jazz films produced by the Goodyear Tire and Rubber Company for distribution in Europe. Left to right: Billy Kyle, Danny Barcelona, Trummy Young, Jewel Brown, Louis, Bill Cronk, and Joe Darensbourg. (April 2, 1962)

Louis Armstrong's life is a screenwriter's dream. Born into stark poverty in turn-of-the-century New Orleans, at his death in 1971 he was perhaps the most widely recognized and genuinely beloved person on the planet. Long after he became wealthy and famous, he lived a down-to-earth life in a middle class neighborhood and gave away much of his fortune. And his existence changed music forever.

Louis always believed that he was born on July 4, 1900 and this date still appears in many reference books. But a baptismal certificate discovered in the 1980s compellingly indicates that Louis was born on August 4, 1901.[1] Why the discrepancy? In rural or impoverished societies in which literacy is not universal, some people do not keep close track of calendar dates. Events are remembered more by phenomena ("the day we had the big thunderstorm and the mulberry

An early incarnation of the All Stars. Left to right: Big Sid Catlett, Barney Bigard, Louis, Earl "Fatha" Hines, Jack Teagarden, Arvell Shaw. Louis's copy of this photo is autographed by each of the band members. Big Sid has written: "To Satchmo, My Pops Armstrong, Good deal, Big Sid Catlett." Teagarden has written: "To 'Pops' Louis, Mama don't wear no dress, from Jack Teagarden. (c.1948)

tree fell down") than by the numbers on a wall calendar. And when little children begin to ask, "When is my birthday, Mama?" they are sometimes told that they were born on a significant date such as Christmas Day or the Fourth of July. This was probably the case with Louis. But the possibility also exists that Louis's mother, Mayann, actually believed that Louis was born on the Fourth of July because — as she later told Louis — she remembered hearing the firecrackers. But what she heard could have been gunshots. As Louis reported in his autobiography, "Mayann told me that the night I was born there was a great big shooting scrape in the Alley and the two guys killed each other."[2] Although the "born on the 4th of July" story isn't true, the patriotic date is appropriate for the man who would transform American music and become America's cultural ambassador to the world.

When Louis was born his parents, Willie and Mayann Armstrong, were living with Willie's mother, Josephine Armstrong, in a neighborhood so tough that it was called "The Battlefield." Louis recalled that, "There were church people, gamblers, hustlers, cheap pimps, thieves, prostitutes and lots of children. There were bars, honky-tonks and saloons, and lots of women walking the streets for tricks to take to their 'pads' as they called their rooms."[3] Soon after Louis's birth, Willie and Mayann separated. Willie went to live with another woman, Mayann moved to a different neighborhood, and Louis stayed with his grandmother. Five years later, Louis reunited with his mother and discovered that he now had a younger sister, Beatrice (conceived during a brief reconciliation between Willie and Mayann), who would always be known by the nickname "Mama Lucy."

Louis discovered music early in life. How could he not? He was surrounded by it. Catholic and Baptist churches, brass bands, funeral parades, piano players in the whorehouses, bands in honky-tonks, string bands performing for dances, the cries of street vendors, the French Opera House, and the music of various immigrant groups were all a daily part of New Orleans culture. Singing hymns was one of Louis's earliest musical memories because his grandmother and great grandmother had taken him to church regularly. At about age seven, Louis — who through his hymn singing and incredible natural gifts had developed a good ear for harmony — and three other

TOP In the Voice of America studios. Left to right: Woody Herman, Bobby Hackett, Louis Armstrong, Barney Bigard, Willis Conover. (July 28, 1955)

LEFT This photo is a reminder that Louis was always a consummate professional who took his work seriously. Louis Armstrong, Tallulah Bankhead, Bob Hope, and Jerry Lewis prepare for a broadcast of "The Big Show," a 90-minute radio program that unsuccessfully attempted to compete with the new medium of television. (December 17, 1950)

OPPOSITE PAGE An arty shot of Louis and the big band. (c. 1940)

boys (Little Mack, Big Nose Sidney, and Georgie Grey) formed a vocal quartet that performed on street corners for tips. Within another few years, Louis took a job working on a junk wagon with Alex Karnofsky, the son in a hardworking family of Russian Jewish immigrants who had taken a liking to little Louis. When on the junk wagon, Louis sometimes blew a little tin horn to attract customers. In an autobiographical manuscript written late in his life, Louis recalled that:

> *After blowing the tin horn — so long — I wondered how would I do blowing a real horn — a Cornet was what I had in Mind. Sure enough, I saw a little Cornet in a pawn shop window — Five Dollars — My luck was Just right — with the Karnofsky loaning me on my Salary — I saved (50 cents) a week and bought the horn. All dirty — but was soon pretty to me.*[4]

Louis, without too much effort, was immediately able to pick out the notes to a popular song of the day, "Home Sweet Home." As the weeks and months passed, he began to develop on the instrument.

On the evening of December 31, 1912, Louis and his friends were in the streets to sing to the New Year's Eve revelers for tips. Louis had brought along a revolver, swiped without permission from his stepfather's drawer, to use as a noisemaker to help celebrate the New Year. Egged on by his friends, he fired the pistol into the air. A policeman standing nearby witnessed the incident and arrested Louis. The next morning Louis — who had possibly been in trouble previously for stealing newspapers and other minor infractions — was ordered into a prison wagon and transported to the Colored Waif's Home for Boys, located just outside the city limits.

Although Louis no doubt missed his freedom and would have much preferred to be back home with his mother and sister, in some ways life at the Waif's Home agreed with him. He thrived on the uniform schedule, regular meals, manual labor, and the emphasis on discipline. But most significantly, he was gradually befriended by Peter Davis, the band director. Louis joined the Waif's Home band, received his first formal instruction in music, and eventually became the leader of the band. When the Waif's Home band played in a parade that traveled through Louis's old neighborhood, the pimps and prostitutes and hustlers in the crowd were so thrilled to see their "Little Louie" leading the band that they passed the hat and collected so much money that the band was able to purchase new uniforms and new instruments. It was an auspicious beginning to Louis's career.

In June 1914 Louis was released from the Waif's Home[5] and, after a brief stay with his father and stepmother, returned to live with Mayann and Mama Lucy. He continued to practice his cornet but, as the breadwinner for the household, the teenage Armstrong also unloaded boats and delivered coal. The great cornetist Joe Oliver, a well-established musician who was in his thirties, recognized Louis's talent and became his teacher and mentor. As Louis's skills developed, he began to perform professionally in bars and parades. When Joe Oliver moved to Chicago in early 1919, Louis replaced him in the Kid Ory band, one of the finest bands in New Orleans. From 1919 through 1921 Louis performed with Fate Marable's orchestra on the Streckfus line riverboats. Working with Marable compelled Louis to improve his sight-reading and introduced him to the decorum necessary to perform for white audiences.

In August 1922 Louis moved to Chicago to join Joe Oliver, by then known as "King" Oliver. Louis understood his teacher's playing so intimately and had developed such an ear for harmony that he could spontaneously create spectacular accompaniments to Oliver's solo breaks. The resulting "dual cornet" breaks astounded their audiences. On April 5, 1923, as a member of King Oliver's Creole Jazz Band, Louis made his first recordings.

Louis gradually came to realize that he was destined for greater achievements than playing second cornet beside his hero, Joe Oliver. In September 1924 he moved to New York City to join the famous Fletcher Henderson Orchestra, one of the leading bands of the era. The jazz world was becoming aware of Louis's genius

ABOVE "The Johnny Cash Show." Louis and Johnny performed "Blue Yodel No. 9," which Louis had recorded with Jimmie Rodgers forty years earlier. (October 10, 1970)

TOP LEFT Louis — as do all master musicians — had great powers of concentration. Note the furrowed brow. (Nice, 1948)

BOTTOM LEFT With Barbra Streisand at the premiere of the motion picture *Hello Dolly*. Louis's 1964 hit recording of "Hello Dolly" was an incentive to create the motion picture. (1969)

TOP Publicity shot of the big band taken soon after Joe Glaser began to manage Louis. (Late 1930s)

and, in addition to recording with Henderson, Louis made recordings with Bessie Smith, Ma Rainey, Alberta Hunter, and Sidney Bechet. But Louis became unhappy with his limited role in the Henderson Orchestra — he was given infrequent opportunities to solo and was rarely allowed to sing — and in November 1925 he returned to Chicago.

Within two weeks after his return to Chicago, Louis assembled a group of musicians, several of whom were former members of Oliver's band, and entered the studios of Okeh Records to make his first recordings as a bandleader. Between November 1925 and 1928 Louis and this group, called the Hot Five (and later the Hot Seven), made sixty-three recordings that today are considered some of the most influential in jazz history. The Hot Five existed primarily as a studio group and seldom performed in public. But Louis was no stranger to the bandstand. He was a featured soloist with the Erskine Tate Orchestra, which played classical overtures, operatic excerpts and other composed music for the silent

films at the Vendome Theatre. He performed with the Carroll Dickerson Orchestra at the Sunset Café and eventually fronted Dickerson's band, which was renamed Louis Armstrong and His Stompers. He also made recordings with a number of singers including Sippie Wallace, Chippie Hill, Lillie Delk Christian, and Nolan Welsh. (Today, these recordings are prized for Louis's contributions rather than the singing.)

In 1929 he returned to New York and soon landed a job in the pit band for the Broadway show Hot Chocolates (music by Fats Waller and lyrics by Andy Razaf). Louis's interpretation of "Ain't Misbehavin'" so thrilled audiences that the number was elevated from the entr'acte in the pit to an Armstrong showcase on the stage. Louis's recording of "Ain't Misbehavin'," as well as

TOP The All Stars arrive in Canada. Left to right: Barney Bigard, Velma Middleton, Cozy Cole, flight attendant, Louis, reporter, Arvell Shaw, Earl Hines. (Probably Winnipeg, c. 1949)

BOTTOM An early incarnation of the All Stars (Louis, Barney Bigard, Jack Teagarden, Earl Hines, Arvell Shaw, Cozy Cole, and Velma Middleton) arrives in Brussels. Lucille stands just above Louis. Pierre Tallerie (a.k.a. "Frenchy"), the road manager, is at far left. (Brussels, 1949)

his recordings of other popular songs such as "I Can't Give You Anything But Love," introduced his talents to a national audience and Louis hit the road. Between 1929 and 1931 the Louis Armstrong Orchestra (which over the years was actually a series of big bands led by Luis Russell, Carroll Dickerson, or Zilner Randolph but for which Louis was always the "front man" and featured soloist) performed in major theaters in Detroit, St. Louis, Chicago, New York, Baltimore, Philadelphia, Dallas, Houston, Memphis, and New Orleans. Louis was now a star.

Beginning in the 1930s, Louis's career became permanently characterized by a whirlwind schedule of concerts, recording sessions, broadcasts and travel. But regrettably, although his music was as superior as ever, his professional affairs were in terrible disarray, chiefly because of a series of inept and even corrupt, mob-connected managers. (During the heyday of Prohibition, mobsters such as Al Capone and Dutch Shultz often controlled the speakeasies in which jazz musicians performed.) In 1932, partly to escape his troubled entanglements, he sailed to London and performed for sold-out crowds. He was surprised to discover that, because of the international distribution of American recordings, thousands of Europeans loved jazz music and especially loved him. When he arrived in Denmark in 1933, he was greeted at the Copenhagen railway station by 10,000 fans. After a series of appearances across northern Europe and back in London, he spent much of 1934 relaxing in a rented apartment in Paris — the longest vacation he would ever take in his entire career. In November 1934 he performed several times at the celebrated Salle Pleyel.

When Louis finally returned to the United States in 1935, he looked up Joe Glaser, the former manager of the Sunset Café (where Louis had performed in the 1920s) and, with a simple handshake, Glaser became Louis's manager. The handshake contract lasted for the rest of their lives. Glaser took care of everything — marketing, bookings, itineraries, payroll, taxes, royalties, residuals, and hiring (and sometimes firing) Louis's backup musicians — all Louis had to do was walk out on stage and play. Under Glaser's management, Louis was transformed from star to household name. When in 1937 he substituted for Rudy Vallee for six weeks as the host of the Fleischmann's Yeast Show, he became the first black American to host a nationally sponsored radio program. He began to appear in feature films such as *Pennies from Heaven* (1936), which starred Bing Crosby, and *Every Day's a Holiday* (1938), which starred Mae West. He continued to tour, perform, and record with his orchestra and he also made best-selling recordings with Crosby, the Mills Brothers, and many others.

By the mid-1940s, the changing musical tastes of the public, the war-time travel restrictions, and the financial burden of transporting and paying seventeen musicians began to make the big band format unviable. Louis was reluctant break up his group because he hated the thought of putting his sidemen out of work. But concerts that he performed with small groups at New York City's Carnegie Hall and Town Hall were so musically and commercially successful that he disbanded the orchestra and formed a septet called Louis Armstrong and the All Stars. Although the All Stars used a somewhat traditional New Orleans instrumentation of trumpet, trombone, clarinet, piano, bass, and drums, the band performed a wide variety of material including New Orleans jazz, show tunes, popular standards, and the occasional novelty number. The All Stars remained together — although the personnel would occasionally change — for the rest of Louis's life. As the group's name connoted, over the decades many renowned musicians performed in the band, including Jack Teagarden, Barney Bigard, Earl Hines, Big Sid Catlett, Cozy Cole, Edmund Hall, Trummy Young, and Tyree Glenn.

TOP LEFT OPPOSITE PAGE
Still from the motion picture *Artists and Models*. Because it was then considered scandalous for a white actress to dance with black cast members, Martha Raye (in the center of photo) wore dark body make-up. (1937)

TOP RIGHT OPPOSITE PAGE
Louis with Takako Suganomiya, the daughter of Emperor Hirohito. (Japan, 1963)

BOTTOM OPPOSITE PAGE
Louis and Lucille being interviewed by Paloma Efrom. (Buenos Aires, 1957)

BELOW Louis's traveling trucks were embossed with his favorite nickname, "Satchmo."

The All Stars followed a sometimes grueling schedule of nightclub appearances, concerts, jazz festivals, recording sessions, film appearances, radio and television broadcasts, private parties, and domestic and international tours. Audiences loved them. During their first visit to Africa in 1956, the All Stars performed at the polo grounds in Accra for a crowd that *Life* magazine estimated at 500,000 people.[6] Most of the audience had hiked for miles just to catch a glimpse of Louis. The African tour was documented by Edward R. Murrow's CBS television show, *See It Now*, and the footage was later edited, combined with additional footage of a tour of Europe and a concert with Leonard Bernstein, and released as the theatrical documentary *Satchmo the Great*. Louis and the All Stars also had a prominent role in the 1956 feature film *High Society*, which starred Bing Crosby, Frank Sinatra, and Grace Kelly.

Louis — who had made his first recording three decades earlier — continued to create music that the record buying public wanted to hear. He had a hit with "Blueberry Hill" (1949) before it was recorded by Fats Domino and struck again with "Mack the Knife" (1955) before it was recorded by Bobby Darin. At the height of rock and roll's British Invasion, Louis's "Hello Dolly" (1964) knocked the Beatles out of the number one slot that they had held for weeks. The song was the title song from a new Broadway musical starring Carol Channing. The producers of the show complained that every week patrons were asking the box office to refund their money because they had arrived at the theatre expecting to hear Louis Armstrong and were upset that he wasn't in the show. Three years later, Louis appeared in the motion picture version of *Hello Dolly* with Barbra Streisand.

LEFT Waiting for the band bus. For every hour in the spotlight, musicians spend countless hours traveling. (1940s)

RIGHT Louis stirs the laundry in a washtub during a tour of the deep south. People without running hot water indoors heated water using a small fire under in a backyard washtub. (Early 1940s)

TOP Charming the studio audience on the Mike Douglas Show. (1970)

By the 1960s Louis was an American cultural icon. He had performed in perhaps every major nation in the world except for the U.S.S.R. and China, had made best selling recordings for five decades, was a frequent guest on all of the top television shows, and had one of the most recognized faces — and voices — on the planet. But the strain of constant travel and life on the road was beginning to take its toll. Louis had suffered a heart attack in Spoleto in 1957, and from then on, at Joe Glaser's insistence, Louis's personal physician always traveled with the band.[7] Louis was hospitalized several times in the late 1960s for circulatory problems, kidney ailments, and heart problems. When, during a medical examination, his physician advised him to stop touring altogether — arguing that because he was already wealthy and famous and had contributed so much to the world, there was no need to jeopardize his increasingly fragile health — Louis, wearing only his boxer shorts, leaped off the examination table, pantomimed playing a trumpet, and exclaimed that he was meant to play music and that he must not let his audience down.[8] Louis accepted a two-week engagement at New York City's famous Waldorf-

Astoria Hotel for March 1971, and his doctor pleaded with him to cancel the booking. Louis stubbornly refused, but then agreed to a compromise. Louis checked into a suite in the hotel. Every evening he took an elevator to the second floor, entered the Empire Room, performed a single set, and then took the elevator back to his room. And every day his physician came by the hotel and gave him a full medical exam. Soon after the Waldorf-Astoria engagement, Louis suffered a heart attack and was placed in the intensive care unit of Beth Israel Hospital. By mid-April he was much improved and on May 6th he returned to his Corona home to recuperate. On July 4, 1971, he celebrated his 71st birthday with a few friends. The next day Louis telephoned his manager and told him to get the band together for a rehearsal. He passed away peacefully in his sleep in the early morning hours of July 6, 1971.

LOUIS THE MUSICIAN

Louis's impact on jazz is beyond measure. Dan Morgenstern aptly observed "there is not a single musician playing in the jazz tradition who does not make daily use, knowingly or unknowingly, of something invented by Armstrong."[9] Those who know of Louis only as a the congenial singer of "Hello Dolly" or "What a Wonderful World" may be startled to learn that he revolutionized twentieth century music.

Louis is often cited as the first great soloist in jazz. Although jazz may have evolved into a soloist's art without him, there is little doubt that his innovations in the 1920s established a new standard that other musicians were then obligated to meet. Jazz in the early 1920s was primarily an ensemble music during which more accomplished performers might venture two-bar or four-bar solos. (Listen to Louis's wonderful two-bar breaks on "Tears," recorded with the King Oliver's Creole's Jazz Band 1923.)

LEFT A rare photograph of the Louis Armstrong Orchestra. Lucille is sitting on the shoulders of drummer Big Sid Catlett. (Mid-1940s)

OPPOSITE PAGE When Louis was discharged from Beth Israel hospital in the late 1960s, many of the doctors, nurses, and staff posed for pictures with him. Louis labeled five of the pictures and inserted them into a scrapbook. Left to right: Dr. Gary Zucker (Louis's personal physician), the President of Beth Israel Hospital, Louis, nurse, Lucille. (Late 1960s)

But with the Hot Five, Louis created chorus-length solos of unprecedented virtuosity and stunning inventiveness. His stop-time chorus on "Potato Head Blues" displays all the daring of a high wire act without a net and his opening cadenza to "West End Blues" is justly famous for its breathtaking originality.

Louis's playing and singing were saturated with that ineffable rhythmic momentum called "swing." Louis swung, and jazz followed him. Listen to "Naughty Man," a recording he made with the Fletcher Henderson Orchestra soon after joining them in November 1924. The other members of the band, including even Coleman Hawkins, who would grow to become one of the greatest saxophonists in jazz, sound stiff and jerky compared to Louis. But then listen to "Sugar Foot Stomp" or "T.N.T." recorded months later. The band, members of which readily acknowledged that Louis had brought a fresh approach, is beginning to swing. Don Redman — who arranged "Sugar Foot Stomp" and who would go onto create classic arrangements for Count Basie, Jimmy Dorsey, and many others — declared that he changed his style of arranging after hearing Louis Armstrong. It is no exaggeration to state that the swing era of the 1930s grew directly out of Louis's conception.

Louis's stunning technical virtuosity astonished both jazz fans and other musicians. His rich, buttery tone, flawless execution, and effortless three-octave range changed the sound of jazz trumpet forever. Even symphonic musicians were compelled to reconceptualize their approach after hearing Armstrong.

Louis was the only figure in jazz — or perhaps all of western music — who was equally significant as a singer as well as an instrumentalist. (As the inimitable Stanley Crouch once said, "It would be like if Beethoven stood up from the piano and started to sing!") The iconic image of Louis is as a trumpet player, but his singing and trumpet playing are of equal artistic weight. Ella Fitzgerald, Tony Bennett, Billie Holiday and many others cite Louis as their primary influence. Louis is sometimes identified as the inventor of scat singing or the first to record scat. He didn't invent it — scat has deep roots in black American culture — and he wasn't the first to record it. But his recordings, especially "Heebie Jeebies" (1926) and "Hotter Than That" (1927) did greatly popularize scat singing and today it is difficult to hear a scat performance without being reminded of Louis (or at least of Ella Fitzgerald, who learned from Louis).

TOP The Hot Five has long been thought to have been solely a recording group. This clipping indicates that the band also performed in public. (Late 1920s)

BOTTOM Louis — hospitalized in Spoleto, Italy, after a heart attack — is obviously bouncing back. (1959)

Louis's prominence as a performer has overshadowed his contribution as a composer. But more than fifty of his compositions are on file at the Library of Congress, and many of them (e.g., "Struttin' with Some Barbecue," "Potato Head Blues," "Gully Low Blues") are today considered part of the jazz canon. Louis was somewhat cavalier about his composer credits. In 1918 he sold "I Wish I Could Shimmy Like My Sister Kate" to A. J. Piron for fifty dollars and reportedly gave composer credit for "Struttin' with Some Barbecue" and other Hot Five compositions to Lil Hardin as part of their divorce settlement.

As jazz absorbed the innovations of Charlie Parker, Dizzy Gillespie, Thelonious Monk, Miles Davis, John Coltrane, and Ornette Coleman, Louis's approach remained remarkably consistent. He refined and deepened his abilities as a sensitive interpreter of material. Although some critics mistakenly perceived his music to be old fashioned, Louis continued to produce recordings of enduring merit. Examples include: Louis Armstrong Plays W.C. Handy (1954), Satch Plays Fats (1955), Ella and Louis and Ella and Louis Again (a series of marvelous duets with Ella Fitzgerald, backed by the Oscar Peterson Quartet, 1956-57), Satchmo: A Musical Autobiography (1956-57) and Together for the First Time (Louis and Duke Ellington's only collaboration in the recording studio, 1961).

BOTTOM LEFT When Louis arrived in a city he was often greeted by serenading local musicians.

BOTTOM RIGHT Judging from Lucille and the band's reaction, they are probably reading about themselves in the local newspaper. Tour of the deep south. (Early 1940s)

Louis was a musical alchemist who routinely transformed mediocre ditties into art of the highest caliber. From "Song of the Islands" (1930) to the often delightful album for children *Disney Songs the Satchmo Way* (1968), Louis always transcended the categories of high art and low art. How else to explain "Tight Like This" (1928) in which a majestic trumpet solo comfortably coexists with novelty song hokum? His recording of "What A Wonderful World" (1968) still thrills listeners today not because of the merit of the composition, but solely because of the integrity of Louis's delivery.

Louis enjoyed popularity unrivaled by any other jazz musician. He made hit recordings for five decades and few of his recordings have ever gone out of print. His music is heard today in television commercials, movie soundtracks, Olympic ice-skating routines, and even space flights. He achieved the loftiest artistic peaks while remaining completely accessible. But Louis's innovations as a trumpet virtuoso, vocal stylist, composer, and popularizer should not overshadow his music's ineffable ability to soothe those who are troubled, to inspire those who are discouraged, and to amplify the joy of those who are cheerful. Listening to Louis makes people feel good. This is the mystical essence of music that transcends centuries and cultures.

[1] The baptismal certificate was discovered by Tad Jones, who was engaged in research for Gary Giddins's *Satchmo* (New York: Doubleday, 1988). *Satchmo* includes an insightful examination of the issues surrounding Louis's date of birth.

[2] Louis Armstrong, *Satchmo: My Life in New Orleans* (New York: Prentice Hall, 1954; reprint, New York: Da Capo, 1986): 8.

[3] Ibid.

[4] Louis Armstrong. "Louis Armstrong + the Jewish Family in New Orleans, LA…" Manuscript 1/5, Louis Armstrong Collection, Louis Armstrong House & Archives, Queens College.

[5] Earlier writers assumed that Louis spent eighteen months in the Waif's Home, but researchers now believe that Louis may have been in and out of the Waif's Home between January 1, 1913, and his final release in the summer of 1914.

[6] No other American has ever received a comparable reception in Africa, including Muhammad Ali, who in 1974 won back the heavyweight title from George Foreman in the unforgettable "Rumble in the Jungle" fight in Zaire.

[7] The physician who traveled with the band was Dr. Gary Schiff. During the 1960s, Dr. Gary Zucker became Louis's general practitioner in New York City.

[8] Oral History Interview with Dr. Gary Zucker, January 26, 1996, Satchmo Collection, Louis Armstrong Archives. Zucker's paraphrase of Louis's words is "Doctor, you don't understand. My whole life, my whole soul, my whole spirit, is to blow this horn. My people are waiting for me; I cannot let them down." Zucker recalls that "And I must tell you that a chill went up and down my spine, I got prickly all over my body, and it was almost like a religious experience."

[9] Dan Morgenstern, "Louis Armstrong and the Development and Diffusion of Jazz," in *Louis Armstrong: A Cultural Legacy*, ed. Marc H. Miller (Seattle: University of Washington Press and New York: Queens Museum of Art, 1994): 95

RIGHT Louis peeks out of the train window while arriving at — or perhaps departing from — a European station.

OPPOSITE PAGE Lucille offers Louis a little taste while on a Yugoslav Airlines flight. This photo is from Scrapbook 32 which documents Louis's concert in Belgrade on April 3, 1959.

II The Louis Armstrong House

Louis's den in 1957. Note the stacks of 78s and LPs, the two tape decks, the turntable, and the collages on the wall. (Photo courtesy of Charles Graham)

In 1942 Louis married Lucille Wilson, a dancer at Harlem's famed Cotton Club, and in 1943 they purchased a simple frame house at 34-56 107th Street in the working class neighborhood of Corona, Queens. Louis lived out of a suitcase — he was typically on the road more than 300 days per year — and had no interest in owning a home. Lucille — who had spent some of her childhood in Queens — discovered the house, purchased it, and decorated it without Louis ever having seen it. In an autobiographical manuscript, Louis described his first visit to the House, returning to Manhattan in the early morning hours after an out-of-town performance and then hailing a taxi to drive him to Queens:

> And me, I've never been to this house before, why I could not tell him anything as far as 'the directions' (etc.) how to get there. So the Cab Driver finally found the house. And when he looked around to the back of the Cab and said to me, O.K. this is the place. One look at that big fine house, and right away I said to the driver "Aw man quit kidding and take me to the address that I'm looking for.[1]

Louis and Lucille soon after their marriage in 1942. This photo was one of their favorites and they made copies and gave them to friends.

After Lucille answered the door and gave him a tour of his new home he recalled that:

> The more Lucille showed me around the house the more thrilled I got. Yea you hear? — I got" (tee hee). Right then and I felt very grand over it all. A little higher on the horse (as we expresses it). I've always appreciated the ordinary good things.[2]

By 1943 Louis was already a superstar. He could have lived in a mansion in Beverly Hills or on an estate on Long Island with a swimming pool in the shape of a trumpet. The fact that he purchased a modest home in a working class neighborhood and lived there without pretension for the rest of his life — while giving away a fortune in cash and gifts — is one of the more profound indicators of Louis's innate humility. With the exception of a house in Chicago that Louis briefly co-owned in the 1920s with his second wife Lil Hardin Armstrong, the Corona house was the only home that Louis ever owned. For Louis, whose New Orleans childhood was spent in a crowded two-room bungalow with a privy out back, the Corona home was a dream come true.

LOUIS'S LIFE IN CORONA

Louis cherished his down-to-earth existence in Corona. In many ways Louis escaped the travails of fame by living an unpretentious life in his neighborhood. He had his hair cut at Joe's Artistic Barber Shop (still in business) two blocks away on 106th Street. The neighbors adored him and were proud to have a celebrity — as well as an artist who had been a hero to black America since the 1920s — living among them, but they respected his need to be treated as a regular guy. Towards the end of his life Louis declared that, "We don't think that we could be more relaxed and have better neighbors any place else. So we stay put."[3] Louis was especially fond of children and when approached by them never hesitated to sign an autograph, make a joke, or offer words of encouragement. When he would return from a road trip, kids would greet the band bus, help Louis carry his trumpet and his suitcases inside, and then Lucille would fix everyone a bowl of ice cream while they watched westerns on television. Louis recalls that, even when eating at The Dragon Seed, his favorite Chinese restaurant, neighborhood kids would surround him for autographs:

> *And by the time our food is being served — the kids of the neighborhood might pass by and look through the window and see Satchmo and Round up all the kids in the neighborhood that Satchmo + Lucille is sitting in the Restaurant, and the whole neighborhood of kids come and as soon as the waiter — bring our food, all of these kids make a bee line in the Restaurant to my table for Autographs. Soo — I still haven't eaten my food' for autographing for the kids. The funny thing about it all — they all must have their names, on their autographs. So by the time I finished' hmmm my food were very cold. So I ate my Fortune Cookies, which read — one read — SOCIAL PLEASURE AND A MOST FORTUNATE FUTURE. The other Fortune Cookie said — YOUR ROMANCE WILL BE A LONG AND LASTING ONE. So we left the Dragon Seed and when we went home Lucille fixed me a beeg Dagwood Sandwich.[4]*

Although they remained in this modest house for the rest of their lives — Louis refused to even consider moving — during their decades in the house Louis and Lucille made many remarkable changes. What was originally a frame, clapboard-sided house quite typical of Queens (an "Archie Bunker house") was completely transformed over the decades by grand, and sometimes gaudy, improvements. The redecorating reflected the combined tastes of Lucille and Morris Grossberg, an interior designer based in Manhattan's Upper East Side. Grossberg had previously decorated the home of Dorothy Davenport, a long-time friend of Lucille who lived nearby. Lucille admired Grossberg's work at the Davenport home, and beginning in the 1950s she used him exclusively for the Armstrong home. Essentially every renovation until Lucille's passing in 1983 was jointly planned by Lucille and Grossberg, with little input from Louis. His role was to enjoy it.

WEEK BEGINNING MONDAY EVENING, JULY 8, 1929
MATINEES THURSDAY AND SATURDAY

CONNIE'S
"HOT CHOCOLATES"
A New Tanskin Revel
WITH

PROGRAM CONTINUED

ENTRE'ACTE
Trumpet Solo by Louis Armstrong

ACT TWO
Scene 1
The Wedding of the Rabbit and the Bear

Hostess .... EDITH WILSON
Bunnies .... PAUL and THELMA MEERES
Bear .... BABY COX
Rabbit .... Madaline Belt
Fox .... Paul Bass
Monkeys .... Mary Prevall, Louise Williams, Natalie Long
Pussy-Cat .... Margaret Simms
Frogs .... Midnight Steppers
Sister Twister .... Louise Cook
Jackass .... Billy Maxey
Zebras .... Bon Bon Buddies
Birds .... Jubilee Singers

Scene 2
Harlem Street Scene
Billy Maxey, Dick Campbell, Frances Hubbard, Pearl Baines

PROGRAM CONTINUED ON NEXT PAGE

LEFT This advertisement for Hot Chocolates was kept in one of Louis's scrapbooks. Note that Louis's feature number, "Ain't Misbehavin'," has already been moved to the entre acte. (1929)

BOTTOM Louis, Charles Graham, and cornetist Ruby Braff visit with Louis in his den. (1957) (Photo courtesy of Charles Graham)

LEFT Louis and Lucille in Louis's den. (Late 1960s)

BOTTOM RIGHT Louis hugs Adele Heraldo, his next-door neighbor. He used to drop in on the Heraldos and ask Adele to make him an egg sandwich. Today, Adele's daughter, Selma — who still lives in the house — is an active member of the Louis Armstrong House & Archives Advisory Board.

BOTTOM LEFT Jack Bradley snapped this photo of Louis and Lucille goofing for the camera in the den. (Photo courtesy of Jack Bradley)

TOP "Joe's Artistic Barbershop" is still in existence at 33-06 106th Street just a short two blocks from Louis's house. (1965) (Photo: John Loengard/Getty Images)

RIGHT One of the last photos ever taken of Louis, this snapshot shows a down-home guy on a summer day. Note the Budweiser hat, cigarette in hand, Band-Aid on the right knee, and the plastic covered couch.

The two story house was built in 1910 by Thomas Daly. When the Armstrongs purchased the house from the Brennans — an Irish-American family who had lived in the house for decades — the house had changed very little. The Armstrongs enclosed the front porch and removed the interior walls of the parlor and front bedroom to create a colossal 70-foot living room. They filled it with comfortable couches and chairs and at one end of the room placed a gorgeous maple console containing a Grundig four-band tuner and turntable. Lucille loved flowers and the ceramic vases in the living room were always filled with cut flowers.

In the mid-1940s, Lucille's mother moved into the second story. The house was originally built as a two-family dwelling and the floor plan for the second story was the same as the first. The second story, accessible via the front hall staircase, had a full kitchen, dining room, bathroom, and two bedrooms. After Lucille's mother passed on in 1949, the Armstrongs gradually began to transform the second floor. The kitchen and back bedroom were renovated into a combination master bathroom and a dressing room. The small parlor was converted into a den for Louis and it truly became Louis's realm. When he was home, this is where he spent much of his waking time engaged in his favorite pastimes of writing, recording audiotapes, and visiting with friends. The rest of the house may have been "Lady Armstrong's," but Louis's den was entirely his own.

Louis was a prolific writer and while at home he wrote at the curved mahogany desk in his den. During his years in the Corona house he completed his second autobiography, *Satchmo: My Life in New Orleans* (1954), and two major articles for *Ebony*, "Why I Like Dark Women" (1954) and "Daddy, How the Country Has Changed" (1961). For *Esquire* he wrote "Jazz on a High Note" (1951) which provided Louis's insights on his most famous recordings and he authored dozens of smaller articles and columns for *Melody Maker*, *The Record Changer*, and other periodicals. He also composed more than two hundred pages of autobiographical manuscript that remained unpublished in his lifetime. Fans would send Louis letters and gifts and every writer received a personal reply. Louis adored his fans and it was not unusual for him to knock out a six-page, single-spaced, typed letter to a fan whom he had casually met backstage only once. Louis was especially fond of green ink and many

ABOVE Louis signs autographs in his backyard. (1965) (Photo: John Loengard/ Getty Images)

TOP OPPOSITE PAGE Louis with his tape collection. He is pointing to one of his 650 hand-decorated tape boxes. (Late 1960s)

BOTTOM OPPOSITE PAGE Louis at his desk in his den with Lucille beside him. Note his Tandberg tape decks on the left and his tape collection on the right. (Late 1960s)

of his letters were written with green ballpoint pens or typed using a green typewriter ribbon. All in all, Louis probably wrote more than ten thousand letters. Historians may never determine which of Louis's writings were created in the den and which were created in hotel rooms and dressing rooms. (Louis traveled with a typewriter from as early as 1922.) But it is safe to state that Louis's den provided him with a sanctuary in which, unencumbered by the demands of concert halls, recording studios, and airport schedules, he was free to engage in his cherished pastime of writing.

Always an enthusiast of technology, shelves of his den held the best available audio equipment — Ampex, or Tandberg reel-to-reel tape decks, Garrard or Dual belt-driven turntables, and Acoustic Research speakers — and there was usually music playing while Louis was in the room. His tastes centered upon traditional jazz and classical music, but Louis — always a champion of melody — was equally fond of shmaltzy, popular music. When reporters would ask the musical genius who were his favorite recording artists, he sometimes shocked them by truthfully responding, "Guy Lombardo."

THIS PAGE Louis on the front steps of his home with neighborhood kids. These photos have become some of the most requested images from the collections of the Louis Armstrong Archives. (Late 1960s)

Although his den eventually held a personal library of more than fifteen hundred 78s, LPs and 45s — including more than two hundred one-of-a-kind acetate discs of airchecks and test pressings — Louis's favorite audio format was reel-to-reel tape. During the 1950s he recorded hundreds of seven-inch reels. Being a frugal man, he recorded many of his tapes at 3-3/4 inches per second (the slowest speed) so that he could store the most material on each reel. What he sacrificed in fidelity — a faster speed would have given him an improved audio signal — he gained in breadth. Because a typical reel contained one to two hours of material, his private tape collection comprised more than one thousand hours of recordings. On some reels Louis dubbed his favorite commercial recordings, including his own. But the remaining tapes contain stunning, one-of-a-kind spoken-word recordings. Louis had an astonishing habit of setting his tape deck to "record" and speaking into the microphone, sometimes for more than an hour. And when he was hanging out in his den with Lucille, friends, neighbors, band members, or whomever, he would also set his deck to "record" and let the tape roll. Participants usually knew that they were being recorded but after a few minutes of visiting with Louis all traces of self-consciousness vanished. During his years in the house Louis taped hundreds of hours of jokes, stories, and conversations. One such tape captures Louis's visit with a man who is obviously professionally involved with audio equipment — perhaps as a salesman or an engineer — and who has dropped by the house to give Louis advice on his audio set-up. Louis is especially proud of his Ampex tape decks ("It's the boss!") and compares them to Selmer trumpets ("Selmer trumpets's better than all the Goddamn trumpets in the world!"). They discuss the respective merits of Tandberg tape decks and Ampex tape decks, and when Lucille enters the room a few minutes later Louis unintentionally fuses the two brand names and proudly announces that he is considering purchasing a "Tampex" deck. Lucille and the guest have a good laugh at this and it takes a minute for Louis to catch on to what was so funny. Louis's little den was filled to capacity with recordings, audio equipment, books, musical instruments, and other accoutrements. In a tape that Louis recorded in 1957, during a telephone conversation with drummer Cozy Cole, Lucille observes that, "We going to have to knock out some walls and extend his den for him," and Louis chimes in that his den, "looks like a whorehouse on Christmas morning!"

RIGHT Charles Graham with Louis's turntable and amplifier. The photo was intended to document Louis's audio equipment, but it also captures Louis's collages on the wall behind. (Photo courtesy of Charles Graham)

LEFT In 1958, the west wall of the den was covered with Louis's collages. (Photo courtesy of Charles Graham)

OPPOSITE PAGE This oil portrait was painted by Calvin Bailey in 1948. He based the portrait on a photograph by Anton Bruehl that appeared in the November 1935 issue of *Vanity Fair*. Louis was especially fond of the Bailey painting, which still hangs today in the living room of the Louis Armstrong House.

Knowing Louis's love of audio technology, in 1958 jazz enthusiast and journalist Charlie Graham decided to write a story for *Hi-Fi Music at Home* (a magazine for audiophiles) about Louis's audio equipment. The resulting article, "He Tapes It All!" provides an entertaining and detailed record of Louis's equipment and how he used it. At the time of Graham's visit, Louis had "two Norelco tape recorders, a Harmon-Kardon preamp and 40-watt amplifier, a Collaro changer, and an Acoustic Research speaker."[5] Graham also observed that Louis "has a small speaker in his bathroom so he can listen to music while shaving and dressing."[6] (There are still speakers in the master bathroom today.) When Graham — accompanied by the great trumpet player Ruby Braff, who modeled his style after Armstrong — came to Corona to interview Louis, he took marvelous photos of Louis's tape decks, turntable, amp, reels of tape, stacks of LPs, piles of 78s, and the other such trappings. But over the years, Graham's photos have proven even more valuable for quite another reason. Although Graham's intention was to document Louis's equipment, he inadvertently photographed the wall behind Louis's equipment. And this wall was covered with of one-of-a-kind collages created by Louis. What a riot of images it is! An 8 x 10 photo of Louis shaking the hand of a smiling, well-dressed boy about 12 years old; a poster from the Apollo Theater that indicates that Louis is headlining there; Lucille and Louis greeting composer W.C. Handy; a headshot of a baseball player; a beauty in a two-piece swim suit; a banner from "Hot Club Düssaldorf; an official portrait of a formal dinner with more the two hundred guests; Louis and the All Stars getting off the plane in Africa; Winston Churchill's face; Lucille in a pretty black and white dress with her legs crossed; Louis, a drummer, and a clarinetist in performance; another bathing beauty; Louis and fans; contact sheets for photos of Louis on a television show; Mannekin Pis, (i.e., the famous Brussels fountain of a little boy peeing); Lucille and Louis sharing a meal; Louis and his big band; still another bathing beauty; Louis, pianist Marty Napoleon and two fans; and a buxom, scantily clad woman with long, flowing hair.[7] Lucille, believing that the collages were in poor taste, removed them while Louis was on tour. Today, Graham's photos are the only detailed record of Louis's wall of collages.

LOUIS'S FINAL YEARS: 1960S-1971

During the 1960s, because of his declining health and the advent of rock and roll, Louis began to spend less time on tour and more time at home. But, as in the old days, it was not unusual for him to return home from a tour to discover that Lucille had redecorated a room.
.

In the guest bathroom Morris Grossberg covered every inch of the walls and ceiling with mirrors and thereby transformed the tiny bathroom into a brilliantly reflective compartment worthy of Versailles. The work was performed by Michael Beal, one of the top mirror technicians in the country and owner of Manhattan Glass and Mirrors. Grossberg topped off the luxurious effect by installing a cream-colored onyx birdbath that had been converted into a pedestal sink and adding gold-plated fixtures imported from Italy. Louis adored the room and a 1971 article in *Time* on celebrity bathrooms, "How the Other Half Bathes," features a photograph of Louis, in his favorite striped bathrobe, proudly standing before the onyx sink in his mirrored bathroom.

OPPOSITE PAGE The Armstrongs removed two interior walls and enclosed the front porch to create a colossal living room.

LEFT Every inch of the walls and the ceiling of the first floor bathroom is covered in mirrors.

The Armstrongs occasionally employed people to help with the upkeep of their home. A hired man named Ernie was with them for many years and became an indispensable part of the household. Lisa Gerkin — a pretty German immigrant whom Louis met when she was a barmaid in the neighborhood — cooked, ironed, and cleaned for the Armstrongs in the 1960s. One day, while the Armstrongs were out, she brought a friend or a relative into the House and had souvenir pictures of herself taken in almost every room. ("Can you believe it? Here I am, working in Louis Armstrong's house!") Her photos show tall ceramic vases filled with cut flowers, chairs covered in leopard print fabric, elegant swag curtains, and a gag toilet seat that is imbedded with real coins.

The Armstrongs had always been fond of entertaining in their backyard, but, as is typical of backyards in Queens, there was little room for more than an outdoor table, a few lawn chairs, and a portable gas grill. Immediately to the south of the Armstrong's home was a frame house that was, by the 1960s, vacant and in disrepair. In 1967 New York City seized the property for unpaid taxes and eventually demolished the house. In May 1971 the City placed the property up for auction and the Armstrongs submitted the winning bid of $10,875. Louis, who was recuperating from a heart attack and had just returned home from Beth Israel Hospital, explained (partially tongue-in-cheek) to a newspaper reporter that, "I'm going to landscape this lot with trees, bushes, and flowers and maybe even a small croquet court. Then I'm going to sit out here and enjoy my garden and maybe even blow my horn a little."[2] The Armstrongs landscaped the 60 x 100 foot lot into a handsome garden inspired by Japanese design. They created a brick surfaced patio and added a small bathroom and a wet bar with cedar cabinets and covered by a cedar pergola. Just off the patio was a small fishpond stocked with real Japanese koi and guarded by an ornamental brass bullfrog. A flagstone walkway wound from the front of the house past two pairs of birch trees to the patio. On the southeast corner of the garden were installed a flagstone deck and two sets of outdoor electrical receptacles so that a combo could perform during parties. The garden was lit by six fixtures in the shape of carriage lamps, and was watered by an underground sprinkler system operated by remote timers. The finishing touch was the addition of a new gas grill, installed in an elaborate wrought iron casing painted white, and fed by an underground gas line. The Armstrongs now had a place to entertain in style.

The final stage in the Armstrong's transformation of the little frame house took place in the early summer of 1971, when they covered the entire house with a brick façade. To save money, the front and garden sides of the house were covered with brick, but the back and alley sides were covered with brick-face stucco. They also built a narrow brick storage shed in the back for garden furniture and tools, and constructed a handsome brick wall with a concrete cap to surround their new garden. Not wishing to be perceived as "putting on airs," Louis offered to cover the house of his next door neighbors, Adele and Selma Heraldo, with brick as well. The Heraldos declined, but did allow the brick masons to extend the brick face along the retaining wall in front of their house.

During the early morning hours of July 6, 1971, Louis passed away peacefully in his sleep in the master bedroom. Lucille immediately called the Heraldos who already sensed that something was wrong because they noticed that the Armstrongs' bedroom lights were on before dawn. Lucille then summoned Dr. Gary Zucker, Louis's personal physician, and Oscar Cohen, his manager at the time. The following morning headlines all over the world announced Louis's passing. On July 8th he lay in state at the Seventh Regiment Armory in Manhattan and more than 20,000 mourners filed past his coffin in twelve hours. His funeral was held on July 9th at the nearby Corona Congregational Church on 37th Avenue. Because the church could hold only a few hundred mourners, most of whom

ABOVE Getting ready to go to work. Note the briefcase that is labeled "Satch." (March 1947)

LEFT Louis sings, "Hello Dolly" to girls from his neighborhood. This photo was taken just two doors from Louis's house. (1965) (Photo: John Loengard/Getty Images)

BOTTOM RIGHT Lucille at the opening of the Louis Armstrong Intermediate School, just blocks from the Louis Armstrong House. Seated immediately behind Lucille is Helen Marshall, at that time a Representative to the New York State Assembly, but later to be President of the Borough of Queens.

BOTTOM LEFT After Louis's passing, Lucille received more than 20,000 letters of condolence, including this one which was addressed simply, "Mrs. Satchmo, Queens, New York, America." It was delivered.

were celebrities and elected officials, 37th Avenue and the surrounding streets in Louis's community were packed with thousands of neighbors, fans, and curiosity seekers. Later that day, Louis was buried in Flushing Cemetery.

LUCILLE'S WIDOWHOOD, 1971-1983

After Louis passed, Lucille received more than 20,000 letters of condolence. They arrived from musicians, celebrities, heads of state, jazz fans, school children, and people who probably couldn't have named an Armstrong record if they had to, but who just liked Louis. A letter from New Zealand was addressed simply, "Mrs. Satchmo, Queens, New York, America" and a letter from Paris was addressed "Lady Louis Armstrong, New York, USA" — the postal service delivered them. Lucille — knowing how much Louis loved his fans and how he always attempted to answer every letter — aspired to reply to each one. Associated Booking (Louis's managing agency) sent Phoebe Jacobs out to Corona to assist Lucille with the overwhelming task of answering the mountain of mail.

Lucille had always skillfully fulfilled the public role of being Mrs. Louis Armstrong. But now that Louis was gone, her role took on an additional dimension. She became in many people's eyes a living link to their departed hero. According to Phoebe Jacobs, Lucille was at first uncomfortable with her new role, wondering why anybody would invite her to give a talk or make a public appearance. But as the 1970s progressed she grew to appreciate how her work helped people to feel close to Louis. Lucille, often accompanied by Phoebe, attended tribute concerts, appeared at unveilings of Louis Armstrong statues and paintings, traveled to Eastern Europe and distributed Louis's recordings to jazz fans, and established an annual Louis Armstrong Scholarship in jazz studies at Brandeis University (Waltham, Massachusetts).

Community and cultural leaders in Queens also searched for appropriate ways to honor their famous citizen. A proposal to rename Northern Boulevard, the principal street through northern Queens, as "Louis Armstrong Boulevard" fizzled out because Lucille thought the naming of a street was an honor too ostentatious for Louis. The ELMCOR community center (a fusion of the neighborhood names "Elmhurst" and "Corona"), sponsor of a drug rehabilitation program and an after school athletic league, developed many of their activities under a program called LAMP, i.e., the Louis

OPPOSITE PAGE TOP LEFT
The stair chair was installed in 1971 to help Louis get to the second floor.

OPPOSITE PAGE BOTTOM RIGHT
The Louis Armstrong House in the late 1950s.

Armstrong Memorial Project. The most widely visible tribute to Louis in his community was the renaming of the Singer Bowl — a performing arts venue in Flushing Meadows Corona Park where Louis had performed during the 1964 World's Fair — as the Louis Armstrong Stadium. The ceremony was held on July 4, 1973, (Louis's birthday) and was an official event of the Newport Jazz Festival-New York. The five dollar admission provided a spectacular, all day concert featuring an incredibly diverse line-up which included Count Basie, Freddie Hubbard, Dave Brubeck, Ella Fitzgerald, Cozy Cole, Sarah Vaughan, Vic Dickinson, Sun Ra, John Mayall, and dozens of others. Today, the Louis Armstrong Stadium is owned by the United States Tennis Association and is part of the National Tennis Center. Each September during the U.S. Open, hundreds of thousands of tennis fans watch world-class matches in Louis Armstrong Stadium. In May 1977 the Meadows Elementary School, located at 34-74 113th Street, just six blocks east of the Armstrong's house, was renamed the Louis Armstrong School, and a middle school with a coveted magnet program in nearby East Elmhurst opened in 1980 as the Louis Armstrong Intermediate School.

In 1977 the Armstrong's home was declared a National Historic Landmark and was entered onto the National Register of Historic Places. On February 21, 1979, the United States Department of the Interior presented Lucille with a bronze plaque reading "Louis Armstrong House, National Historic Landmark, 1977," which was prominently affixed to the front of the house.

In 1978 Lucille made a drastic alteration: she plopped a third floor onto the top of the house. The third story was a self-contained apartment that included a sitting room, a bathroom, bedroom, and a walk-in cedar-lined closet. Her intent was to have an apartment so that a live-in caretaker or a close friend could share the house with her as she got older and, presumably, more infirm. The design and construction of the third floor was undertaken with little or no consultation from an architect or engineer. Nor did Lucille file any required papers with the Queens Department of Buildings. If she had, the project would never have been approved as a three-story frame structure was — and still is — illegal in Queens. And Lucille either did not realize or chose to overlook the fact that alterations to a national historic landmark should be reviewed by the State Historic Preservation Office. As might be expected, the third story was poorly designed and constructed, with the ill-fated result that Lucille had progressive leaks throughout the lower stories from then on.

In early October 1983, Lucille traveled to Brandeis University for the presentation of the Louis Armstrong Scholarship. Minutes before she left home, she met with Bessie Williams, her longtime, trusted housekeeper. For the first time ever, she gave Bessie an extra set of keys to the House and asked her to "Take care of the place while I'm gone." (Lucille's words would prove prophetic — Bessie continued to work in the House until her retirement in 2001.) Lucille suffered a heart attack during the trip and passed away on the morning of October 13th. She was buried in Flushing Cemetery next to her husband. The preservation of Louis's home would now enter a new phase.

CREATING A HOUSE MUSEUM

After Lucille's passing, the administration of the Armstrong estate became the responsibility of David Gold who had been appointed executor under Lucille's will. Gold was also president of the Louis Armstrong Educational Foundation, Inc., a not-for-profit private foundation that had been in existence since 1969. (The official brochure of the Louis Armstrong Educational Foundation explains that, "In 1969, Louis Armstrong funded and founded the Louis Armstrong Educational Foundation stating, 'I wanna give back to the world some of the goodness the world gave me."[9]) Gold and Phoebe Jacobs (who became Vice President of the Foundation) were faced with many critical decisions concerning what to do with the Armstrong House and its contents. They arranged for Bessie Williams to continue her regular maintenance of the House. Lucille's will stated that the House was to be given to the City of New York to be operated "in respectful memory of my deceased husband."[10] In 1986 Gold and Jacobs arranged for the House to be given to the New York City Department of Cultural Affairs and for the House to be administered by Queens College under a long-term license agreement. Also in 1986, the New York City Landmarks Preservation Commission designated the Armstrong House, because of its cultural significance, to be an official city landmark.

LEFT Before the Armstrongs purchased the lot next door, they entertained in a small backyard.

OPPOSITE PAGE TOP LEFT Louis Armstrong House, circa 1965.

OPPOSITE PAGE TOP RIGHT The great bassist Milt Hinton snapped this photo of Louis with his tape decks and turntable. Note the trumpet on the couch and the photo of Lucille taped to the inside of the truck's door. (Photo courtesy of the Milton J. Hinton Photographic Collection) (1950s).

© 2003 Benedetto Arts

TOP LEFT Tony Bennett/Anthony Benedetto. "Louis Armstrong," oil on canvas, 23 x 19.5 inches. Tony Bennett recalls that, I painted a portrait of Louis and presented it to him in London. He took one look at it and said, "You out-Rembrandted Rembrandt!" — a classic example of his great and unique sense of humor. I heard he hung the painting in his study and when anyone visited him and asked him who painted it, Louis would say, "Here's a painting a boy from my neighborhood did of me." (Courtesy of benedettoarts.com)

TOP RIGHT Holiday dinner at the Armstrongs. Far left: Lucille; third from left: Clarence; to right of turkey carver: Doc Pugh, Louis's valet; far right: Velma Middleton. (1960s)

BOTTOM LEFT This is the same group that has assembled for the Holiday dinner. Clarence is seated on the floor on the left. Louis has his portable tape deck ready to record. (1960s)

TOP The west wall of the dining room is entirely covered with a floor to ceiling mirror.

BELOW The Armstrongs enjoyed a state-of-the-art kitchen that included a six burner, double oven, double broiler stove that was custom made for them.

The project to turn a vacant private home into a historic house museum was more complicated than anyone imagined. The 1.6 million dollars required for design and construction was supplied by the Borough of Queens, the Save America's Treasures Program, and the National Endowment for the Humanities. In 1998 Rogers-Marvel Architects completed a master plan and in 2001 Buttrick, White and Burtis Architects finished the design. The bulk of the project was restoration and conservation — Louis's den was restored to look exactly as it did during his final years in the House (Lucille had altered it slightly in the 1970s), and wallpapers, upholstery, and other materials that had deteriorated over the decades were replaced in kind. Only three substantial changes were made: the illegal third floor that Lucille added in 1978 was removed, the garage was renovated into a modest Welcome Center, and a basement laundry area was renovated into a handicapped accessible public bathroom. In October 2003, the Louis Armstrong House opened to the public as a historic house museum. If Louis were to magically return to this world and see that his little house was a museum, visited by thousands of people each year, he would no doubt be very surprised.

THE ARMSTRONG HOUSE TODAY

Because no one has lived in the Armstrong House since Lucille's passing, visitors to the Armstrong House today see it very much as it was during the last years of Louis's life. The living room is still comfortably furnished with couches and chairs arranged in convenient conversation groups. A cream colored spinet piano rests along the inside wall, although there is little evidence that Louis himself played it, and a Sony Trinitron color television sits in a mahogany cabinet, behind closed doors when not in use. At the west end of the room hangs an oil portrait of Louis by Calvin Bailey, based on a photograph by Anton Bruehl that appeared on the cover of *Vanity Fair*. A companion portrait of an elegantly dressed Lucille, painted by Count Lee, is displayed on an adjacent wall. Near the windows, at eye level for those seated on the couches, hangs an original LeRoy Neiman oil portrait of the great baritone saxophonist Gerry Mulligan. Louis discovered it at an art sale at the New York Armory in Manhattan and purchased it on impulse. Above the piano is a vibrant pen and ink sketch of the conductor Arturo Toscanini, who in many ways was a contemporary of Louis's. The entire effect of the living room is one of elegance and comfort.

THIS PAGE & OPPOSITE PAGE Lisa Gerkin, who worked as a maid for the Armstrongs, apparently had a friend take souvenir photos of her in various rooms of the house. Today her photos provide handy documentation of how the Armstrong House looked in the 1960s. Note the gag toilet seat imbedded with coins. (Photos courtesy of Lisa Gerkin)

Lucille and Morris Grossberg loved decorative finishes and over the decades they covered every wall with eye-catching papers. Even the interiors of the closets, including the ceilings, are papered in colorful patterns that do not appear anywhere else in the house. The master bath and dressing room — and the insides of the cabinets and drawers — are totally covered with shiny, silver foil paper. The living room and hallways feature a beige, textured "sea grass" paper; the kitchen and breakfast nook are papered with a restful, Asian-inspired, cherry tree motif; and the tiny guest room on the second floor is covered with a psychedelic orange floral design that exactly matches the fabric of the room's daybed. The basement recreation room at one time was covered with a vibrant, blue, tropical fish and bubbles design (a pattern that would not have been out of place in a child's room), but it was papered over in the 1970s with a wild, yellow and reflective silver wallpaper that complements the faux leopard skin carpet on the basement stairs.

The kitchen was totally renovated in the early 1960s to include custom cabinets finished in brilliant turquoise lacquer. Hidden snugly inside the cabinets are a double set of five-foot-high swinging pantry shelves and two Lazy Susans. The Crown Company sold the Armstrongs a gas range with six burners, two ovens, and two broilers — on the front is an engraved steel plate that reads, "Custom-made by Crown for Mr. & Mrs. Louis Armstrong." Other top-of-the-line appliances include a colossal Sub-Zero refrigerator, which they covered with turquoise panels to match the cabinets, and a Nutone food processor flush-mounted in the counter. Everything is state-of-the-art for the time period. Even the floor's egg-shell white linoleum has been cut and laid in a unique pattern of concentric squares. But this kitchen was not just for show. Louis and Lucille both loved to eat and to entertain. The pantry was always well stocked with food and guests to the Armstrong's home never left hungry.

LEFT Louis Armstrong House, circa 1987. Note the brick façade and the illegal 3rd floor.

OPPOSITE PAGE TOP Louis always had the finest audio equipment. Here he adjusts the record level on one of his Tandberg tape decks.

OPPOSITE PAGE BOTTOM In the spring of 1971 the Armstrongs covered their clapboard sided house with a brick façade. The work was performed by Sebastian Murer. (Photo courtesy of John Murer)

In Louis's den his curved, mahogany desk and his desk chair covered in peach colored leather still sit in the center of the room. Directly behind the desk are mahogany cabinets containing Louis's Tandberg tape decks, Crown power amplifier, and Dual turntable. Facsimiles of his 650 tape boxes line the shelves (the originals are safely housed in climate controlled stacks in the Armstrong Archives) and the dry bar is stocked with jiggers, highball glasses, and silver-plated bar paraphernalia. One can almost hear Louis say, "The house may not have the nicest looking front. But when one visit the Interior of the Armstrong home' they see a whole lot of comfort, happiness + the nicest things."[11]

THIS PAGE & OPPOSITE PAGE These photos were taken at "Joe's Artistic Barber Shop," which is two blocks from Louis's house. Louis inserted the two photos into a scrapbook and labeled them "My Neighborhood Barber" and "My Neighbors." (Late 1960s)

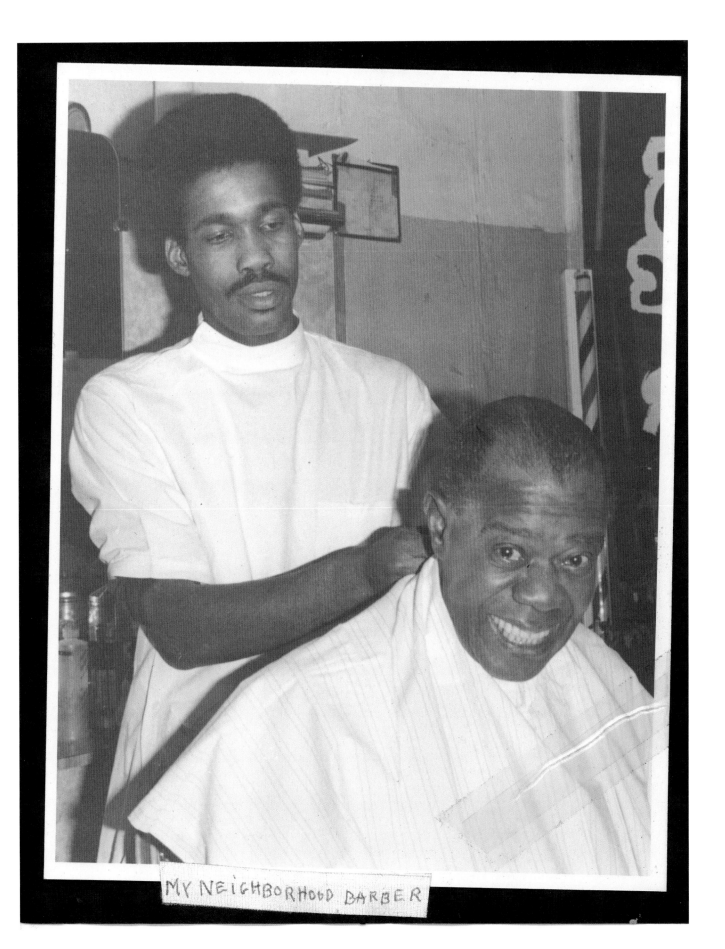

MY NEIGHBORHOOD BARBER

LEFT The Armstrongs covered their little dressing room with silver foil wallpaper.

BOTTOM Louis wrote in his manuscripts that he enjoyed having "a wall to wall bed," i.e. a king-sized bed.

OPPOSITE PAGE The Den was really Louis's realm. When he was home, this is where he spent much of his time.

[1] Louis Armstrong, Untitled manuscript, Manuscript 1/4, Louis Armstrong Collection, Louis Armstrong Archives, Queens College.

[2] Ibid.

[3] Ibid.

[4] Louis Armstrong, "Our Neighborhood," Manuscript 1/11, Louis Armstrong Collection, Louis Armstrong Archives.

[5] Charles Graham, "He Tapes It All!," Hi-Fi Music at Home (March 1958): 43.

[6] Ibid.

[7] These are merely the images that I have been able to discern. Many more are indistinguishable due to the focus of the camera and the glare of the tape with which Louis covered them.

[8] Bernard Rabin, "Satchmo Can't Annoy Next-Door Neighbor," Daily News (May 27, 1971)

[9] Informational brochure of the Louis Armstrong Educational Foundation, Vertical file, Louis Armstrong Archives. The Louis Armstrong Educational Foundation has always been one of the major funders of the programs and services of the Louis Armstrong House & Archives. The Foundation also funds many other worthy programs including Jazz at Lincoln Center, Columbia Center for Jazz Studies, Jazzmobile, and Beth Israel Hospital.

[10] Lucille Armstrong will, Personal Papers, Satchmo Collection.

[11] Louis Armstrong, "Our Neighborhood."

OPPOSITE PAGE TOP Louis in his den in the 1960s. The gold records on the wall are for "Hello, Dolly" and "Mack the Knife." (Photo by Jack Bradley)

OPPOSITE PAGE BOTTOM Today the beautiful garden of the Louis Armstrong House is used for special events, such as our annual children's concerts. Clarinetist Joey Cavaseno (back to camera) makes the kids smile.

RIGHT Phoebe Jacobs, Vice-President of the Louis Armstrong Educational Foundation, assisted Lucille with correspondence, personal appearances, and other duties during the years after Louis's passing.

III The Louis Armstrong Archives

Lionel Hampton and David Gold (President of the Louis Armstrong Educational Foundation) cut the ribbon to open the Louis Armstrong Archives. (May 24, 1994) (Photo: Nancy Bareis)

Visitors enjoy the "What's New" exhibit at the Louis Armstrong Archives on December 10, 2001.

When David Gold and Phoebe Jacobs visited the Armstrong House after Lucille's passing in 1983, they discovered that the little Corona home was overflowing with a treasure trove unlike anything else in the jazz world. The question before them was what to do with it. They arranged for the jewelry, furs, the Armstrong's 1969 blue, four-door Cadillac Fleetwood Brougham, and other personal property to be auctioned in an estate sale by William Doyle Galleries on October 2, 1985. Gold and Jacobs could have easily sold Louis's reel-to-reel tapes, photographs, scrapbooks, gold records, big band arrangements, and autobiographical manuscripts as well — the estate would have made small fortune — but they appreciated that these materials held immense historical significance. After investigation, they realized that Queens College met their criteria as a repository: The College was located just minutes away from the Armstrong House, was building a magnificent new library with a six-room archival suite, and was home to a nationally recognized school of music that was expanding its curriculum to include jazz studies.[1] On December 22, 1986, the Louis Armstrong Educational Foundation donated what is now called the "Louis Armstrong Collection" to Queens College under the provision that the College preserve it, catalog it, and make it available to the public.

In July 1991, Queens College hired me to serve as Curator of the Louis Armstrong Archives.[2] I spent three years processing the mountain of material and on May 24, 1994, the Louis Armstrong Archives officially opened to the public. The very next day, we had researchers arrive at 10 a.m., and they have been coming ever since. Our exhibits and programs in the Archives draw from two major collections: the Louis Armstrong Collection — i.e., Louis and Lucille's own materials donated by the Louis Armstrong Educational Foundation — and the Satchmo Collection — our steadily growing collection of newly acquired Armstrong items.

CHAPTER III

LOUIS ARMSTRONG COLLECTION
HOME-RECORDED TAPES

One of the most fascinating discoveries in the Archives is Louis's collection of home-recorded tapes. In addition to the tape decks in his home, Louis traveled with a steamer trunk that had been modified to hold one or two reel-to-reel tape decks and a turntable so that he could listen to music while he was relaxing in the dressing room or hotel room. As Louis was using state-of-the-art technology to carry his favorite music with him wherever he went, his bulky trunk packed with audio equipment can best be imagined as a "1950's Walkman." Louis transferred music from hundreds of 78 RPM discs and LPs in his personal collection onto reel-to-reel tape so that he could listen to music on the road. Tape was his format of choice because he could carry up to several hours of music on one 7-inch reel, whereas carrying stacks of heavy 78s was cumbersome and dangerous to the fragile discs. More than 200 of Louis's 650 tapes contain dubs of favorite commercial recordings and are of immense interest because they document what the master musician listened to for pleasure. Guy Lombardo, Erroll Garner, Glenn Miller, Bunny Berigan, Tchaikovsky, Jelly Roll Morton; it's a diverse list of recorded sound. Italian pop singer Ray Martino was a particular favorite. But one unifying characteristic on these tapes is the prominence of melody. Louis was a disciple of melody and prized a strong melody delivered in a straightforward manner. This explains Louis's aversion to bebop — he once declared that the boppers "play all them notes that don't mean anything." In Louis's aesthetic, melody was paramount and "running the changes" (a jazz musician's term for improvising upon a given chord structure in a workmanlike manner) held no merit.

Louis's tape collection is also notable in that dozens of the reels are dubs of Armstrong's own commercial recordings. It is common for musicians — whether jazz, classical, or pop — to shun listening to their own work. But Louis was unusual in that he routinely listened to his own recordings purely for pleasure.

Just as Louis did with his tape decks in his home, while in the hotel room or backstage dressing room he would hit the "record" button when he was hanging out with band members, visitors, or whomever. At least one hundred of Armstrong's reels capture dressing room visitors swapping jokes and stories, musicians sharing candid tales of racial discrimination and other travails of life on the road, Louis warming-up before a performance, Louis reminiscing into his tape recorder, Louis being interviewed by reporters, and other such events. Louis relished a dirty joke well told and dozens of these tapes capture backstage joke swapping sessions.

One tape captures a 1952 visit in the Dunbar Hotel in Los Angeles between Louis and Stepin Fetchit (the stage name of Lincoln Perry), the great actor and vaudevillian whose dim-witted, "Uncle Tom" style endeared him to stage and screen audiences for decades but also doomed his career when his type of character became widely perceived as racially offensive. The little group in the hotel room is obviously having a party — there is howling laughter over silly things — and the tape candidly captures two great artists just hanging out. Among the banter, Perry and Louis sometimes touch upon serious

ABOVE Louis traveled everywhere with a trunk that was modified to hold his tape deck and turntable. Think of it as a "1950s Walkman."

RIGHT This photo of Louis was taken by the great bassist — and photographer — Milt Hinton. (Photo courtesy of the Milton J. Hinton Photographic Collection)

matters. Louis complains that accountants are deducting from his payroll $800 for taxes. Louis urges Perry to accept more film roles — at this date he had made more than thirty films but his career was waning — and tells him, "Every move you make...you're just a born movie star." Perry mentions that he has been approached to portray Satchell Paige, the great pitcher in the Negro Leagues, in a motion picture and Louis encourages him to pursue it. But the bulk of their visit is devoted to swapping dirty jokes, each trying to outdo the other. Louis takes the prize with an account of a wealthy woman who offers to give her new Cadillac to a man if he will perform an obscene act with her. He considers this for a moment and then replies, "Is the car filled up with gas?"

Many of the tapes capture Louis practicing his trumpet or playing along with the radio or recordings. One tape — a perennial favorite of visitors to the Armstrong Archives — captures Louis playing his trumpet along with a 78 RPM recording of "Tears," a disc he made with King Oliver's Creole Jazz Band in 1923. Louis explains, "I thought you would like to hear the difference in recording between the old and modern recordings." Then he drops the needle onto the spinning 78 disc, and, as the music of "Tears" fills the room, he picks up his trumpet and plays along. It's a fascinating juxtaposition. To hear the 1923 performance of "Tears," a performance well known to all Armstrong fans, accompanied by a musically vital Louis Armstrong in the late 1950s, highlights just how long and vibrant a career Louis enjoyed. On the disc's penultimate chorus, young Louis took a series of two-bar stop-time breaks. While making the tape, a much older Louis answers the breaks with two-bar trumpet interludes, creating an overall effect of a Louis Armstrong solo pattern of 1923-1950s-1923-1950s, etc. At the end of the performance, Louis announces the names of the musicians on the disc and then declares, "I wanted you to hear how this had been Satch-u-ated. Get it?"

Not only did Louis record more than 650 reels of tape, he also cataloged the contents of his tapes. The Archives contains three separate tape catalogs: two are written by hand and one is typed. Louis most likely created these catalogs during the last years of his life, when he had more time off the road. This is evidenced by the fact that all of the handwriting is uniform in style and ink, as if Louis wrote the entries sequentially over several weeks rather than individually as he recorded each tape over the years. On listings, he would typically cite artist and titles for recorded music and the persons present for candid talk sessions. He typically concluded each listing by writing either "More" (i.e., "see next page for more contents") or "S'all," (i.e., "that's all on this tape"). He also created three indexes of his tapes. The most curious one is an index of titles arranged by last word. In this index "Do Nothing 'till You Hear from Me" is filed under "Me," "On the Sunny Side of the Street" is filed under "Street," etc. For Louis, a genius who never finished the fifth grade, this index was a valiant attempt to gain control of his ever-growing tape collection, but for visitors to the Archives today, it is enjoyed as a wonderfully idiosyncratic document.

COLLAGES

Not only did Louis record 650 reels of tape and catalog their contents, he decorated almost every one of his tape boxes. Just as Louis had at one time decorated the wall of his den with collages, he clipped photographs, telegrams, postcards, news clippings and other found material and assembled them into collages on the front and back of the seven-inch square boxes. Louis then carefully laminated the collages with Scotch tape. Because at least five hundred of Louis's tape boxes are decorated, front and back, the tape box collection encompass more than one thousand collages. The extent of Louis's collage work was not generally known until Queens College began to process the Armstrong Collection and remains today an overlooked facet of Louis's oeuvre.[3] Historians knew that Louis was an instrumentalist, vocalist, actor, writer, etc., but had

THIS PAGE The Louis Armstrong Archives has three of Louis's passports. This one, issued in 1957, provides a cornucopia of data on where Louis was when. Louis was photogenic, and even his passport photos look great. (Photos: Lisa Kahane)

ABOVE Reel 140. Front: "Mr. Joe Glaser and his Dear Mother, Mrs. Bertha" (Louis always called Glaser, "Mr. Glaser," so perhaps it's not surprising that he refers to Glaser's mother as "Mrs. Bertha.") accompanied by Louis and Louis with Velma Middleton.
Back: Some of the tape boxes, such as this one, display contents of the tapes. The snapshot is of the All Stars. (Photo: Lisa Kahane)

ABOVE Reel 141. Front: Mezz Mezzrow and friends enjoy a meal in Paris. Judging from Louis's writing, the music on the tape includes compositions by Richard Strauss, Niccolo Paganini, and "Frank Ceasar," i.e. Belgian composer and organist César Franck.
Back: A newspaper cartoon that praises Louis's manager, Joe Glaser, "America's Entertainment Impresario." (Photo: Lisa Kahane)

ABOVE Reel 162. Front: Christmas card from President and Mrs. Richard Nixon. "Delaney and Satch" refers to a taped conversation between Charles Delaunay, the French writer on jazz. Back: Christmas card from Joe Muranyi, the clarinet player in the All Stars. Joe's son, Paul, tries to play Louis's trumpet. (Photo: Lisa Kahane)

ABOVE Reel 26. Front: "How to Listen to Music " indeed. and the 'Old Timers" refers to Louis's early recordings with King Oliver and Fletcher Henderson. Back: Louis and Lucille. Clarence Williams (pianist and composer) seems to be wearing Velma Middleton (the All Stars' vocalist) as a necktie. (Photo: Lisa Kahane)

little inkling that he was also a visual artist. A 1953 Armstrong letter in the Archives indicates that Louis was already making collages: "Well, you know, my hobbie (one of them anyway) is using a lot of scotch tape...My hobbie is to pick out the different things during what I read and piece them together and making a little story of my own."[4]

Louis's collage work offers yet another angle of vision into the mind of a creative genius. The art of collage is much like the art of jazz: found material is divided into components and then rearranged to create new meanings. Louis's collages often display multiple layers of meaning that are more intuitive than deliberate.

The tape box for Louis's Reel 163 shows a smiling Armstrong, eyes raised to the heavens, dressed in a tuxedo and holding his trumpet and trademark handkerchief. But surrounding Armstrong are three additional smiling Armstrong faces, identical to the embodied one. Louis must have possessed four identical photos which he then clipped to create the collage.) The overall effect is a sort of joyful weightlessness as Armstrong and his accompanying smiles float on the tape box. In the upper right hand corner is written "$3^{3/4}$," the tape speed in inches per second. Handwriting in the top center provides Louis's tape number and a clue to the contents: "Reel 163, opara [sic] — singing, Milt Hinton Combo." (Milt Hinton was the great bass player who performed with Cab Calloway, Duke Ellington, and many others including Louis, and who lived in Hollis, Queens, not too far from Louis and Lucille's home.)

One of the more elaborately constructed collages on the tape boxes is the one on Louis's Reel 68. Louis cut-up promotional flyers and newspaper reviews of a 1959 concert he performed at the Hollywood Bowl and affixed them to a tape box to create a stunning collage which is visually more exciting than any of the original materials alone. Especially interesting is how Louis incorporated the various reds and yellows of the found materials onto the red background of the tape box.

The collages on the box for Tape 473 feature a June 24, 1971, headline from *The Register* in Orange County, California, that reads "Satchmo Talking in His First Interview Since His Illness: 'Tell All the Cats the Choirmaster up there in Heaven will have to wait for old Louis'" and a headline from June 25, 1971, *The Miami Herald* that reads, "Satchmo Bouncing Back, Eager to Work Again." What makes these collages especially bittersweet is the realization that because Louis passed away on July 6th and these headlines had to have been published, clipped, and mailed to him cross-country, Louis must have pasted them onto this tape box during the very last days of his life.

Tape boxes were not the only recipients of Louis's collages. He also filled a scrapbook solely with collages. Scrapbook 20 in the Armstrong Archives contains more than two-dozen elaborate, colorful collages. Many of the collages explore elements of black American culture in the 1950s. For example, one collage includes a photo of vocalist Billy Eckstine and bandleader Count Basie shooting pool, accompanied by the caption "A million dollars worth of talent," the smiling face of pianist and vocalist Nat "King" Cole, and a photo of the popular vocal quartet The Ink Spots, accompanied by the caption, "Negroes who Work on Broadway." The overall effect is one of pride and respect tempered by the whimsy of collage.

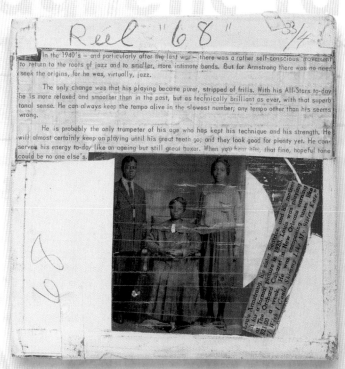

ABOVE Tape Reel 68. Louis has incorporated red promotional materials for a 1959 concert at the Hollywood Bowl onto the red tape box. The back shows the well-known photo of Louis, his mother, and his sister c. 1922. (Photo: Lisa Kahane)

ABOVE Reel 12. Front: English vocalist Beryl Bryden. "Armstrong's personal recordings" indicates that the tape is of Louis's own commercial recordings. Back: "Taken at Catherine and Count Basie's swimming pool, at his birthday party, August 1969." (Basie lived in St. Albans, Queens, not far from Louis.) (Photo: Lisa Kahane)

ABOVE Reel 61. Louis loved kids and saved many photos of children he had met. Louis's use of white adhesive tape produces a novel framing effect. (Photo: Lisa Kahane)

ABOVE Reel 66. Front: The snapshot is labeled, Mrs. Stella Oliver, wife of Joe King Oliver (and) Louis Armstrong (in New Orleans). Louis recorded their visit. Back: The All Stars, circa 1953: Velma Middleton (vocals), Barney Bigard (clarinet), Billy Kyle (piano), Milt Hinton (bass), Trummy Young (trombone) and Kenny John (drums). (Photo: Lisa Kahane)

ABOVE Reel 38. Front: The juxtaposition of Louis holding a napkin to his mouth — he looks like he just burped — placed above a sexy photo of Jane Mansfield is somehow very funny. Back: Louis in Europe, 1950s. (Photo: Lisa Kahane)

ABOVE Reel 51. Front: "Chicago comedian Allen Drew gets rinse after 'process.' Hair is then placed under electric dryer — as for women." Back: Louis and fan, 1950s. (Photo: Lisa Kahane)

ABOVE **Reel 76.** Front: Along with Louis (upper left) and the All Stars (bottom) this tape box has an actual sample packet of the herbal laxative Swiss Kriss. Back: Louis and Lucille share a meal with the co-composer of Louis's hit "Blueberry Hill." (It is possibly Vincent Rose.) (Photo: Lisa Kahane)

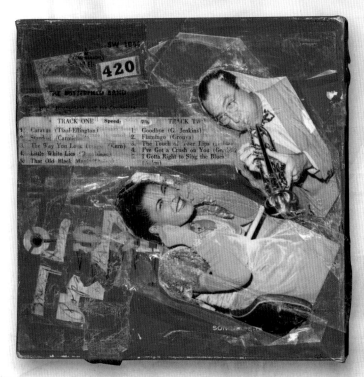

ABOVE **Reel 420.** Front: The red of the tape box contributes to a somewhat wild collage. Back: Louis in a tux, Jesus on his knees in prayer, and Swiss Kriss (the herbal laxative that Louis championed). (Photo: Lisa Kahane)

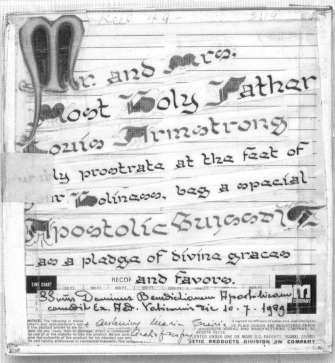

ABOVE Reel 49. Louis has apparently taken a printed blessing mailed from the Vatican, cut it up, and assembled the pieces into collages on the front and back of this tape box. The dovetailing that results in "Mr. And Mrs. Most Holy Father Louis Armstrong" is unintentionally funny. (Photo: Lisa Kahane)

ABOVE Decorated box for an empty reel, i.e, the tape is blank. Front: Clockwise from upper left: Louis and fan pose with the album Satch Plays Fats; Louis in France; Louis on stage with Trumy Young behind him; and clarinetist Edmund Hall and friend. Back: The lady in the upper left is unidentified, but Louis has dubbed his two companions "Snazzy" and "Jazzy." (Photo: Lisa Kahane)

ABOVE Reel 67. On the front of the box Louis has affixed a congratulatory telegram from Otis Rene (the co-composer of "When It's Sleepytime Down South") and a greeting card message. The collage on the back includes in the upper left a photo labeled "Leave it all Behind You," a reference to Louis's belief in laxatives. (Photo: Lisa Kahane)

ABOVE Reel 1. These headlines applauding that Louis had been released from the hospital were published on June 24 and 25, 1971. Because Louis passed away on the morning of July 6, 1971, this box is likely the last box that he decorated. (Photo: Lisa Kahane)

LEFT This entire collage is constructed from photos and news clippings of Jackie Robinson, who broke the color barrier in major league baseball, Robinson lived in St. Albans, Queens, not far from Louis. (Photo: Lisa Kahane)

RIGHT Collage includes (counter clockwise): J. Finley Wilson (Grand Exalted Ruler of the Improved Benevolent Protective Order of Elks of the World) in front of the U.S. Capital; Hall of Fame ballplayer Monte Irvin (New York Giants and Chicago Cubs); a disembodied hand; Shelly Winters, Maxine Sullivan; Kermit Parker, "Governor of Louisiana" (although he was not governor of Louisiana); and Duke Ellington. (Photo: Lisa Kahane)

LEFT This collage from Scrapbook 54 includes (counter clockwise): a photo of "George Walker and Aida Overton Walker, Famed Cake Walk Team"; an unidentified man greeting Louis; "Alexandre Dumas, French mulatto …who authored the Count of Monte Cristo"; a photo of Babe Ruth's farewell speech which Louis has labeled, "Babe Ruth's Last Stand"; the sheet music to "I'm from Milwaukee"; a note from Lucille that reads, "You are the light of my life, I'll love you forever, Your Wife. Brown Sugar"; and a photo of Lucille that has a little Louis head ("Satchmo") in her forehead. (Photo: Lisa Kahane)

LEFT Louis has surrounded himself with the musicians Bunny Berigan, Bix Bieder- becke, Judy Garland, Jelly Roll Morton, Florence Mills, Bing Crosby, Duke Ellington, Jack Teagarden, Ruth Brown, and Big Sid Catlett. King Oliver, Louis' teacher and mentor, is in his forehead. Franklin Delano Roose- velt, the only non-musician in the collage, seems to be listening to Louis's trumpet. (Photo: Lisa Kahane)

RIGHT For Mardi Gras 1949 Louis served as King for the Zulu Social Aid and Pleasure Club, the oldest and most prestigious black krewe in New Orleans. He filled this scrapbook page with photos, his membership card, lists of past Zulu kings, and the exact route of the parade. (Photo: Lisa Kahane)

Another collage depicts a page-size Louis Armstrong head playing a trumpet, surrounded by the much smaller faces of Duke Ellington, Bing Crosby, and other Armstrong associates. In the center of Louis's forehead floats the face of Joe "King" Oliver. The symbolism here is quite transparent. Louis's musical world included many superb colleagues, but King Oliver, Louis's beloved teacher and mentor, would always be central to his thoughts.

ABOVE The Ink Spots ("Negroes who work on Broadway"), Nat King Cole, Billy Eckstine and Count Basie ("A Million dollars worth of talent") assembled into a collage that reflects racial pride. (Photo: Lisa Kahane)

Back of tape box for Reel 163. The three floating heads — Louis must have had four identical photos on hand — create a delightful effect. Note that the tape's contents include operatic arias and music by the Milt Hinton Combo. (Photo: Lisa Kahane)

AUTOBIOGRAPHICAL WRITINGS

One of Louis's favorite pastimes was writing. Louis's published autobiographies and magazine articles were already well known to jazz fans but discovered in the Archives were more than 350 pages of unpublished autobiographical manuscript. (Some of these manuscripts eventually appeared in Louis Armstrong: In His Own Words.⁵) Louis's writing displays a captivating, stream-of-consciousness style that is musical, witty, and full of the joy of life. Consider this opening passage from a manuscript he titled, "Barbershops," written during the last year of his life:

In my neighborhood where I live in Corona, I have (2) Barber Shops. I can get my Hair when ever I want to. The Soul Barber Shop closes on Mondays (rain or shine). My Spanish Barber Shop never closes, except, only on Sundays. Sometimes, if I just have a Hair Cut on a Monday, and just can't wait until the next day, I will make a bee line to the Spanish one, and they are just as glad to have me, anyway. It's just that I'll give ole Soulee the Benefit of the doubt any way. And we Soulees speak the same languages — slanguages — the usual B.S. — talk loud — etc. And they both just knocks me out.

And what's so nice about the whole thing even those Spanish Barbers, they are all from the Old Countries (their countries), their countries somewheres in this world. And they all remebered me when I was touring all over the world — blowing my little trumpet — singing and entertaining them, which they're very happy to remind me of it. Just think — since those days they all (most of them) have married and have big families, and have instilled in their children's mind how they enjoyed Louis Satchmo Armstrong's music. And their kids should do the same.

The entire passage leaps off the page with rhythm. Words and phrases are repeated and developed just as Louis does with melodic motives during a trumpet solo ("they are all from the old countries [their countries], their countries somewheres in this world") and concluding phrases clearly serve as musical cadences ("And they both just knocks me out"). The casual reader may not be consciously aware of Louis's use of repetition, rhythm, and meter, but every reader immediately responds to the delightful, down-home, sentimentality. Louis is one of the most prominent celebrities of the 20th century music ("And they all remembered me when I was touring all over the world"), yet he is thrilled to have two barber shops in his neighborhood so that he can get his hair cut at convenient times ("I can get my hair [cut] whenever I want to"). And there is no doubt that the proprietor and patrons of the barbershops were always glad to see him. In the concluding passages of "Barber Shops," Louis describes what was probably a typical visit for him:

Speaking of this little Spanish Barber Shop, they had a whole Rack of the Spanish albums, which they keep in a corner of the shop. They were recorded down in Miami, Florida and are on sale for anybody who would like to buy one. They're recorded by the finest Spanish singers there is. The price is (90¢) for each album. Sitting right next to me in this shop waiting to get his hair cut also — he and I struck up a conversation about Music and Records, etc. — and I told him about my love for Spanish music and asked him to do me a favor and pick out one of those albums for me, especially the one that he enjoyed listening to the most. Oh, he was very happy to do that for me. He picked the album which was recorded by LOS EXITOS DE ARMANDO. A real beautiful one. And [they] can really sing good. As soon as they finished cutting my hair — I went right straight home (my house) which was just around the corner from the Barber Shop — and recorded the whole album on my big Tape Recorder. Gave it an Index Number and everything.

The LP he mentions was not located among the recordings in the Armstrong Archives (although "Los Exitos de Armando" is probably a title, not a performing group).

Armstrong aficionados have long known that Louis was a prolific letter writer. Visitors to Louis's dressing room or hotel room or even nightclub kitchen would often discover him pecking away at his typewriter. Over the decades, he wrote thousands of letters to fans, friends, and family. Although some of these letters have made their way to the collections of the Institute of Jazz Studies, the Library of Congress, and the William Ransom Hogan Archives, today the bulk of these letters probably are still held by the recipients or their descendants. The Armstrong Archives holds twenty letters discovered in the Armstrong House, most of which were addressed to Lucille. This letter, undated but probably written in the 1960s and penned onto stationery from the Howard Johnson's Motor Lodge in Bordentown, New Jersey, gives insight into the hassles experienced by a professional musician "on the road," and also displays Louis's playful affection for Lucille:

TOP With one hand on his tape recorder, Louis enjoys a late night — or perhaps early morning — snack. His bathrobe is monogrammed "LDA" for "Louis Daniel Armstrong." The presence behind him of an empty bottle of Labatt's Pale Ale indicates that he may be in Canada.

LEFT In his dressing room during a European tour, Louis autographs a photo for a fan. Visible in the left of the photo are three trumpet mouthpieces: one in his horn and two in the case.

Dear Lou, "My Darling"

I forgot to give you this address before I left there. So busy waiting on Rupert the bus driver. At That, he didn't show up. Another Driver Came who was a worker Around the Garage with a Bus Just like the ones' on Northern Boulevard. With a Meter 'N' everything. No Toilet or Anything. Oh' well' That's the Sh-t we've been getting from Rupert + his company All the time. Only Ira + our Office haven't been picking up on it until this time. This old driver did the best' he could. We only had 45 minutes to check in our Hotel – grab a bite' and get back into the bus And Haul Ass to the Job which was (12) Miles from where we lived. We were supposed to hit at 7:30, we arrived at the place at 7 O'Clock' rushed and dressed, ready'.'So, we hit at (9:35,) WOW   WOW. Whatta Gig. It seems that These Cats that's running the Place which is a very nice place, Just don't know what they Are doing. So I see where we're Just have to go Along with them for ten days. Myron Cohen is on the Bill And sends his very best to you. I will at least get a good rest here anyway. The Audience appreciated us very much. Now for the address.

MR. WILEN LANGENBERG
45 BACHLAAN
HILVERSUM HOLLAND
NETHERLANDS.

That's it.
Love you madly. Will Dig you Subsequently
Ol, Sackreface,
Armstrong
P.S. Hope + Dot enjoy you Alls' Freakest Out fitts. (Tee Hee.)

Perhaps the most stunning of Louis's writings discovered in the Archives is his catalog of jokes.[6] He valiantly typed his prized jokes onto pages of low "Satchmo" stationery and compiled the loose leaves into a three-ring binder. He explains why in his "Forward" [sic]:

First I want to say that it's all in fun... And that's all there is to it This book which I've gone to all of this trouble to write in my spare moments — moments when I could be up in the other band boys dressing room — Shooting Craps — or playing a little 'Black Jack (that's, all I play) for my money anyway...tee hee — anyway — I even taken up those precious moments to write these Jokes...Jokes that I've heard from time to time And thought it a good idea to write them down into a book sos that my good friends whom probably haven't seen some of them would get a kick out of seeing them in print... Maybe some of these Jokes might be one of their Jokes[6]...And I know that must be a real Kick to them....

The Foreword itself is a lengthy, totally captivating, stream-of-consciousness account initially composed after returning home from a performance. Louis recalls that, on the return train trip, he ran into the tap dance duo of Pops and Louie, old friends from his early years in show business.

It's actually real early in the morning...I've just gotten in off of the road playing those hard ass one nighters...And since I've already 'slept my ass off on the train coming from Boston (while 'Smiley and the rest of the boys of my Tribe (my orchestra) engage in a little friendly game of Poker...(Ol "Pops and Louie) that marvelous dance team boarded the same train we 'were on as we passed through Boston...We all practically from the same family (as we all say in show "Biz) you can imagine the swell time we all had when we all "Lay eyes on each other...Louie and I had a long Chat in our seats...Pops stood around the boys in the Porker Game...I don't know for sure whether he got into the game or whether he was Just — 'Swollowing a few "Bets...Ha...Ha...

Louis goes on to praise the many musicians and entertainers who contributed jokes to his book, and by doing so confirms what musicians and jazz insiders have always known: jazz musicians have an extraordinarily rich culture of humor.[7] He especially cites Big Sid Catlett, Earl Hines, Zutty Singleton, and, somewhat incongruously, Officer Kelly of the Bridgeport Police Force. Actor and dancer Bill "Bojangles" Robinson "contributed quite a few funny jokes and 'Gags'":

What fascinates me about Bojangles is how he warms up before he goes on the stage before every show...He always has a funny story to tell anyone whom's standing near the Wings, or the stage hands doesn't make any difference as long as he has somebody to tell them to...And they're so dam funny until — if you're on his bill you'll kinda hang around (you know?) casually to hear one of his good Ol good ones before he goes on...I used to go onstage before Bill Robinson...And I was down stairs on the stage before he'd come down...ha..ha...Some other Act before him would be on...Yessir — Bill Robinson and Stepin Fetchit are my Two Choice "Spade Actors"

Louis digresses to tell of an incident during a gig he shared with Louis, Earl Hines, and Zutty Singleton. The setting is Chicago, and although Louis doesn't cite it, the time period is probably the late 1920s. Louis relives the excitement as he types the story:

So anyway — we gave this dance and everything was going along real swell...And along about Intermission time — you know how the Hall usually gets, half Crowded — some of the dancers might go out to get a little "Nip — or "Something that we weren't Selling...cleanout to the door way....So we (Earl — Zootie and myself) were sitting there on the bandstand just talking over different subjects and, etc, — when in walks an old Drunken Darkie — with his shirt tail all stickin out and he was as "Raggity as a bowl of "Slaw...Of course we didn't pay him any attention (much attention) when he entered the hall...But when that 'Back "Sommitch 'reached down into his Pants, a pulled out a great big '45 calibre Pistol....Ump Ump Ump.....Folks you never saw a bunch of ''Niggers run So fast in all your life as we did that night getting out of that dance hall.....Goodness Gracious....And when the Nigger pointed that big ass pistol towards the bandstand towards — Mee — Earl — and Zootie — Lawd Ta'day — It was "Onn — I'm telling 'ya — It was "Onn.......Honest to God — Earl Hines tried his damdest to go through that Upright Piano he was playing...haw haw haw...And poor Zootie — I don't know "Where his Drums went when the Crowd "Crowded the bandstand...Because "Hee — certainly wasn't with them....haw hawhaw...And as for me — 'Shit...I sat on the sidewalk waiting for those Two Boys (Earl — Zootie) asking them why they stayed so long....haw haw haw....Oh Boy...Whata night that was....Ask Zootie and Earl about that incident if ever you run across them....Now you can see how much I have in common with Earl and Zootie....Outside our musical sessions together....More than another Musician I know of....

After composing the extensive Foreword which is so rich in detail, Louis arrives at the heart of the project: transcribing his favorite jokes. Most are ones that were told to Louis by others — he confesses that "there's just a few Jokes in this book that I really could call my own" — and the jokes don't read as if they are in Louis's voice. His joke catalog comprises eighty-seven leaves and contains approximately two hundred jokes, limericks, humorous stories, and poems. Most are far too dirty to reprint in this book. But, because a description of Louis's joke book would be grossly incomplete without at least a few examples, here are some of the cleaner ones. (Remember that the fun of a dirty joke is in the telling.)

CENSUS TAKING

A Census taker stopped at a house... Pressed the button, the door was opened — A Microscopic slit and a feminine voice shrilled — "What is it?"...The man stated his business, when the woman said that this was very embarrassing as she was a Nudist..."Oh — that is all the same to me — I have seen everything" replied the gentleman...Thus — he was permitted to enter — and her statement of utter Nudity was amply verified..."Now — as to your family and the members thereof," said the man..."Well," she responded, "I have my Third Husband — with the First I had Four Children — with the Second — Three Children — and now with my Third Husband I have Two"..."Madam" said the man, — "You're not a Nudist — you just haven't had time to get dressed...

WHO AM I?

Last year I asked her to be my wife and she gave me a decidedly negative reply, so to get even I married her mother...Then my father married the girl...When I married the girl's mother, the girl became my daughter, and my father married my daughter, so he became my son...When my father married my daughter, she became my mother...if my father is my son and my daughter is my mother, who am I?...My mother's mother is my wife and must be my grandmother, and being my grandmother's husband, I must be my own grand-father...And there you are.........

NEW ORLEANS HAPPENINGS

Twenty years ago I was meandering along the spacious Canal St. in New Orleans (my home town) — I noticed a crowd had formed on the opposite side...I hurried across and found it was in front of an Alderman's office and a Trial was in progress...A young man had robbed his lady companion of Eighteen dollars...Just as I entered — the Alderman asked the young dame to explain how the whole thing happened — and she proceeded as follows...I was out driving my Father's Car — this young man, whom I had met only casually shortly before, came walking along — when I observed him I drove up along the curb and invited him to take a ride with me — we proceeded out of town. I drew up and parked under a spreading shade tree — and there is where he took the money... "Where did you have your money?" — asked the Alderman... "In my stocking" replied the Dame...Why did you permit the young man to reach up under your address? I hadn't the faintest suspicion that he might be after my 'money — replied the maiden...The youth was fined "Eighteen dollars and "Cost and the Case was dismissed......

Mixed in with the jokes and humorous stories are eight verses of "The Signifying Monkey" (a traditional black American toast), the lyrics to "Ain't it the Truth" (which Louis has labeled "Song featured by Louis Armstrong In the film — Cabin in the Skies"), and a "Nine Days Diet Chart" (which Louis later reproduced and passed out to friends and fans). Curiously, at least a dozen entries are not jokes or humorous stories at all. The twenty-third Psalm is entered as "A Prayer to You," and typed by itself on a single page is:

OUR MARRIAGE.
Closer and Closer We Shall Grow.
Heart To Heart By Loving So,
Till When The Lights Are Burning Low,
End of Loving And Life And Woe,
Father's Love Will Let Us Go,
As One to Love That Angels Know...

Autographing a book, probably his first
autobiography, Swing That Music. (Late 1930s)

The entire book is completed by an index. Perusing the index of punch lines and joke titles is almost as funny as reading the jokes (use your imagination):

BOOKS

The Louis Armstrong Collection holds more than one thousand books and periodicals. The information to be gleaned from these items is not as self-evident as that from the primary materials such as Louis's spoken-word tapes or manuscripts. But for the astute researcher, Louis's collection of books can provide insightful glimpses into his character.

There is no doubt a story behind Louis's acquisition of each book but the researcher must guard against making false assumptions. Because Louis owned a copy of Jeanette Eaton's biography of Gandhi (written for young readers), does that mean that Louis was interested in Gandhi? Well, maybe so or maybe not. But what is more likely, judging from the presence in the book collection of Eaton's biography of Will Rogers and her later biography of Louis Armstrong, all in the same publisher's series, is that Eaton sent complimentary copies of the Gandhi and Rogers biographies to Louis so that he could sample her work.

But other books offer more substantial evidence. There are two copies of *Ask Your Mama*, a book of jazz-inspired poetry by Langston Hughes, one of which is autographed, "To Louis Armstrong, to whom this book is dedicated with affection and high regard, Sincerely, Langston Hughes." Does the presence of *Interpretation of the Ultraviolet Spectra of Natural Products*, an organic chemistry textbook by Professor A.I. Scott of Yale University, indicate that Louis was a chemistry buff? No, it was an unsolicited gift to him on his 70th birthday. The clue is the author's inscription inside the fly leaf: "Dear Mr. Armstrong, This book was dedicated to you & Willis Conover in 1964 in gratitude for the many hours of pleasure your playing & singing have given me — especially during the writing of the book. Best wishes on your 70th birthday. Perhaps I will write another book for your 80th year as The Master of Jazz. A.I. Scott, Yale University." Sure enough, behind the title page is the printed dedication page reading, "To W. Conover and L. Armstrong."

But did Louis read all of the books in his collection? Did he have favorites? There is little hard evidence one way or the other. One notable exception is the two-volume set of J.A. Roger's biographical dictionary *World's Great Men of Color*. Discovered inside the book were four memo pad sheets on which Louis had carefully printed each chapter that he wanted to read ("Marcus Garvey," George Washington Carver," Jack Johnson," etc.) and then crossed out the chapters that he had read. Ironically, there is no chapter on Louis in Roger's book.

RIGHT Everybody enjoys posing for the camera — especially when Louis is in the picture. (1940s)

OPPOSITE PAGE Kelly Field Airbase, early 1940s.

COMMERCIAL RECORDINGS

In the Louis Armstrong Collection are more than 1,200 commercially issued LPs, 78s, and 45s. Fewer than 350 of these are recordings made by Armstrong. There could be many reasons for this: Perhaps Louis didn't assiduously collect his own recordings, or he gave them away after copying them to tape (his format of choice). Perhaps Lucille gave many away after Louis died.

But what is especially interesting is the variety of recordings in Louis's personal record collection. Louis was a great fan of black comedians and there are worn-out copies of party records by Jackie "Moms" Mabley, Dave Turner, Pigmeat Markham, and Redd Foxx. (For you younger readers — Redd Foxx made these records when he was a stand-up comic notorious for his blue language, decades before the television show "Sanford and Son".) There is a set of 78s by Rafael Mendéz, who is described on the jacket as the "World's Greatest Trumpeter." There are a dozen autographed 78s from E.T. Mensah, the African highlife musician — no doubt he presented these to Louis during his initial tour of Africa.

TOP LEFT Louis Armstrong Orchestra onstage with a tap dancer. (1930s)

TOP RIGHT On the radio in Vancouver, British Columbia.

RIGHT Louis has obviously just told a good joke. This photo perhaps raises more questions than it answers: Who are the patrons? Where was the photo taken? (1940s)

Louis's recording of "Laughin' Louie" (1933) begins with a comically hesitant trumpet solo interrupted by peals of laughter. Experts have speculated that the inspiration for "Laughin' Louie" may have been "The Okeh Laughing Record," a novelty record popular in the late 1920s that also featured a hesitant trumpeter and infectious laughter. The experts are correct: Louis's record collection has three worn-out copies of the "The Okeh Laughing Record."

In his 1966 interview with Richard Meryman, Louis recalled that as a young man in New Orleans, "Big event for me then was buying a wind-up Victrola. Most of my records were the Original Dixieland Jazz Band — Larry Shields and his bunch. They were the first to record the music I played. I had Caruso records too, and Henry Burr, Galli-Curci, Tetrazzini — they were all my favorites. Then there was the Irish tenor, McCormack — beautiful phrasing."[12] In Louis's record collection today are single-sided Victor 78s by Enrico Caruso, Amelita Galli-Curci, and Luisa Tetrazinni, perhaps the very discs that he proudly acquired as a teenager.

BIG BAND PARTS

Louis fronted a big band from the early 1930s until 1947. Apparently, after Louis broke up the big band to form the All Stars, he carried the seventeen cases of manuscript band parts into his Corona home and placed them in a closet. There they sat for almost fifty years. Each musician in the big band had his own case that held his parts. Each case is constructed of black pressboard with brass corners and latches, and on the front, embossed in gold letters, are "Louis Armstrong Orchestra" and the corresponding musician's chair ("1st alto saxophone," "2nd tenor saxophone," etc.).

The Louis Armstrong Orchestra's "book" (jazz musician's slang for the band's library) contained 270 titles. Many of the titles will be familiar to lovers of Armstrong's recordings — arrangements for "Struttin' with Some Barbecue," "Swing That Music," and other notable compositions recorded by Louis and his big band are all present. But there are also arrangements that Louis performed on the job but never recorded, including "Take the A Train," "Do Nothing 'till You Hear from Me," and "Perdido," all titles associated with the Duke Ellington Orchestra.

Almost all of the parts were written by hand — there were only thirty-one stock arrangements discovered in the cases — and about half of these were copied by a professional music copyist. (Today, with the advent of sophisticated computer software for creating scores and printing parts, music copy work is rapidly becoming an obsolete art.) Louis probably had little role in creating these arrangements. The usual procedure would be for an arranger — probably a band member who was paid extra to do so — to create a score. Then the arranger, using the score as his guide, would either copy out the parts himself or give the score to a music copyist to create professionally transcribed parts. Only a handful of arrangements display any indication of who created them. As is common practice in big bands, each part has a number written prominently on the top of the first page, so that musicians can quickly retrieve and file parts by number rather than title — a process that prevents the delay and confusion that would result if on-stage musicians had to alphabetically file titles such as "Lover," "Lover Man," "Love Me or Leave Me," and "Love Walked In."

For the most part, Armstrong's big band book is filled with dependable, straight ahead, swing arrangements that did not rival the creative depth of those played by the bands of Duke Ellington, Count Basie, Benny Goodman, etc. They instead provided a perfect foil for Louis Armstrong to come on stage and dazzle everyone with his virtuosity and his love for the audience. Less than fifty per cent of the arrangements even have a part for Louis — either he never had one or didn't keep one.

Some of the finest arrangements in Louis's book were created by Chappie Willet, who also created swinging arrangements for Gene Krupa, Cab Calloway, Jimmy Lunceford and many others. (The brilliant tap dancer Honi Coles believed that Willet's arrangements were especially great for dancers.) The recordings that Louis made of Willet's charts for "Struttin' With Some Barbecue" and "Swing That Music" remain classics from Louis's big band years. The Armstrong Archives contains a marvelous photograph of Chappie penciling notes onto a score. He is obviously hard at work — his tie is loosened, his vest is unbuttoned, and his shirt sleeves are rolled up to his elbows. An art deco desk lamp provides the required illumination, and mounted on the wall just inches behind him is a rotary pencil sharpener, an essential tool of the trade. He autographed the photo, "Working like this is really a pleasure when its for King "Louie," the greatest of the Great, 'Chappie,' 1940."

Also discovered in the pressboard cases were ephemera (guitar strings, music store receipts, postcards, etc.) that the musicians had in their cases when the orchestra disbanded. Some of these items provide voyeuristic glimpses into the personal lives of traveling musicians. One such example is the presence of three love letters written to alto saxophonist Don Hill. Each letter explores identical themes — "You never write me," "You never call me," "Why haven't I heard from you?" — but, each letter is from a different woman.

RIGHT Chappie Willet created some of the finest arrangements in the library of the Louis Armstrong Orchestra, including "Struttin' with Some Barbecue."

TOP This photo of Louis with young ladies selling stamps is especially interesting because it shows the band-side of the music fronts. One can see the hand-copied music parts, lights, and the necks and mouthpieces of saxophones and a clarinet. (1940s).

RIGHT "And the sound comes out here..."

THIS PAGE AND OPPOSITE PAGE
Louis adored his fans and was never too tired or too busy to have his picture taken with them. The Louis Armstrong Archives has more than two hundred such pictures because Louis saved them.

At the Louis Armstrong Archives, we sometimes allow visitors to touch Louis's trumpets. We decided upon this curatorial policy after realizing that there are dozens of photos of Louis allowing fans to hold his horns. We think Louis would approve.

Louis, being somewhat of a pack rat, saved more than 5,000 photographs. His photo collection includes a wide array of formats from various sources: publicity shots, concert photos, photos that fans snapped and mailed to Louis, images that photojournalists took and presented to Louis, candid snapshots of Louis at home or backstage or in the dressing room, family photos, Louis and Lucille as tourists, etc.

The collection includes more than two hundred nightclub photos. In the 1940s and 1950s, it was not uncommon for a nightclub to have a roaming professional photographer who would take pictures of the patrons, develop the pics on site and insert them into a colorful cardboard sleeve that displayed the nightclub's name, and then sell the souvenir pictures to the patrons. These photographers loved Louis — he was photogenic and he was genuinely thrilled to have his picture taken with his fans, which meant easy business for the photographers. Photo after photo shows a beaming Armstrong backstage with all sorts of folks: high school kids on prom night, Ma and Pa in the big city for a show, hipsters with goatees and turtlenecks, little kids, girls in fabulous hats, and smiling grandparents. There are die-hard Armstrong fans who are thrilled to be standing next to their idol. There are elected officials and other notables who are taking advantage of the "photo op" (a word not coined until decades later); some are obviously tickled to be standing next to Armstrong, and others are, just as obviously, going through the motions. But there is one overwhelming consistency: Louis loved posing for the camera with his fans.

Louis compiled a marvelous collection of more than two hundred photos of other performers. More than fifty of these are autographed to Louis. Especially in the early decades of his career, when he appeared on stage as part of a star-studded evening or when he performed in front of a studio audience for a live radio broadcast, Louis would swap autographed publicity shots with other artists on the bill. (The Armstrong Archives holds autographed photos from the other artists and it's a safe assumption that the other artists received autographed photos from Louis.) Many of the photos provide a fascinating glimpse into the now extinct worlds of black vaudeville and early jazz. A gorgeous studio portrait of the male and female dance duo "McCain and Ross" is autographed, "To 'Louie' Armstrong, the 'High King' of Swing, with best wishes for your continued success, with whom it was a great pleasure to work, sincerely, McCain & Ross." The photo is apparently from the early 1930s. Their best wishes for Louis's "continued success" bore fruit, but McCain and Ross, like the vast majority of performers in any genre and from any decade, never made the big time. A similar story can be surmised from the photo of Pete & Orelia. The photo is a crisp studio portrait by James Kriegsmann, a well-respected photographer of black entertainers (he took at least one notable portrait of Louis), and the photo exhibits Kreigsmann's characteristic use of bright light and crisply defined shadows. A beautiful female dancer in a feathered costume reaches her hands to the sky, and in the foreground three male dancers/drummers, wearing African face paint and heavy strands of beads confront the camera. The autograph reads, "To Mr. Armstrong, 'a mellow fellow,' Pete & Orelia." Where are they now? What a show they must have put on! And you can bet that Louis, that "mellow fellow," enjoyed it heartily.

Louis's collection of photos from colleagues also includes the famous. A publicity shot of trumpeter Henry "Red" Allen is autographed, "To a real genius, Louis (King) Armstrong, from Henry 'Red' Allen" and is dated September 18, 1930. Allen had been a member of Louis's back-up orchestra (i.e., the Luis Russell Band) since the year before. That Red Allen refers to Louis as a "real genius" and "King" should be no surprise. Allen's fate seemed to be to follow in Louis footsteps: he was born in New Orleans six years after Louis, he performed with King Oliver, Clarence Williams, and Fate Marable after Louis performed with them, and by 1929 he was being marketed by Victor records as the next Louis Armstrong. He enjoyed a long and fruitful career, and he and Louis, who collaborated on several memorable recording sessions, always loved and respected one another. The 1930 photo provides incontrovertible evidence of Allen's reverence for Louis.

RIGHT Trumpeter Red Allen was sometimes promoted as "the next Louis Armstrong." He has lovingly autographed this photo "To a real genius, Louis (King) Armstrong, from Henry 'Red' Allen."

In 1956, Louis and his band appeared in the motion picture High Society with Bing Crosby, Frank Sinatra, and Grace Kelly. It would be Grace Kelly's final film before she left Hollywood to marry the Prince of Monaco and become Princess Grace. She bestowed upon Louis who — judging from letters that he wrote at the time — was astounded by her beauty, a Metro-Goldwyn-Mayer publicity shot. She signed it in her elegant script, "To Satchmo – My best wishes, Grace Kelly." Each year thereafter, Louis and Lucille received a Christmas card from the Principality of Monaco. The cards continued to arrive at the Louis Armstrong House well until the 1990s, years after Louis's and eventually Lucille's passing. (Yes, the Armstrong Archives has saved them.)

A publicity shot of the comic actor Nicodemus Stewart, dressed in tattered clothes, holding a battered felt hat in his hands, and gazing covetingly at a cigar butt on the pavement, is autographed, "To Alpha and Louis, Long swing the King with his Queen, From Nicodemus." (Alpha was Louis's third wife about whom more is written later.) Nicodemus typically portrayed shuffling, dim-witted characters in the manner of Stepin Fetchit and Willie Best. He is best known today for his appearances in the motion pictures *Cabin in the Sky* (1943) and *Stormy Weather* (1943), and especially for his role as the janitor Lightnin' on the television version of Amos 'n' Andy in the 1950s. Louis also appeared in *Cabin in the Sky*, but his screen time was limited to a single scene.[13] Nicodemus didn't appear in this scene so it's possible that Louis and Nicodemus never saw each other on the M-G-M set. Exactly where and when Nicodemus gave this photo to Louis is an unanswered question.

For every jazz musician who became a household name — such as Louis Armstrong or Duke Ellington or Ella Fitzgerald — there were hundreds of others who never achieved comparable fame, but who were highly regarded by their peers and by jazz aficionados. Louis's photo collection often documents these musicians and their working conditions. A photo taken at Tony's Tavern, a Chicago hot spot, on Valentine's Day in 1935 shows, as the caption reads, a "party in honor of Duke Ellington and Louis Armstrong" and the knowledgeable viewer will easily spot in the left of the photo Louis and Duke sitting together. (Armstrong aficionados will also recognize Alpha on Louis's left and across the table is Clarence — Louis's adopted son. More about Clarence and Alpha later.) But the photo also shows, somewhat scattered amongst the many guests, a pianist, guitarist, and trumpeter who are apparently engaged as the

TOP Louis and Grace Kelly appeared together in the motion picture *High Society*. It was Kelly's last picture before she married the Prince of Monaco.

ABOVE In the early 1930s, shops in New Orleans sold a Louis Armstrong cigar. Louis kept one of the bands in a scrapbook.

TOP RIGHT "Party in honor of Duke Ellington and Louis Armstrong at Tony's Tavern...February 14, 1935."

house band at Tony's Tavern. A second photo taken three weeks later shows only the house band. It's the same pianist and trumpet player as in the Ellington-Armstrong celebration, but with a different guitarist and now a drummer is visible. A professionally printed sign hanging above the piano reads "Little Joe Lindsey and His Orchestra," an overly grand description of the quartet. (It's possible that the photo captured only four members of a bigger band.) Yes, the band is led by drummer Joe Lindsey, who in New Orleans was one of Louis's closest buddies — he and Louis formed a band together while they were teenagers. The photo is autographed, "To Louis Armstrong, Best wishes from Joe Lindsey + Orch." and Louis wrote on the photo, "Tony's Tavern, Chi[cago] – March 4, 1935." A hand-lettered sign reads, "Don't forget to feed the kitty," an unsubtle reminder that the band appreciates tips. This is not a renowned seventeen piece orchestra performing for the floor shows at Chicago's legendary Regal Theatre (a venue which was sumptuously decorated with sparkling chandeliers and rhinestone studded curtains); this is a group of local musicians performing in a neighborhood tavern on — as the date confirms — a Monday night. Perhaps the photo was a poignant reminder to Louis that none of the musicians that he ran with in his younger years was enjoying the success that he was.

SCRAPBOOKS

Of the eighty-five scrapbooks in the Louis Armstrong Collection, more than one dozen of them were assembled by others and presented to Louis, usually to commemorate a concert or tour. Typical of these is a scrapbook that displays a label on the front that reads, "Cairo, United Arab Republic – January 28, 1961." It is filled with 8 x 10 black and white photos of Louis visiting tourist's spots, chatting with local celebrities, and other off stage activities. In one photo, Louis is offered a plate of kebobs, which he eyes somewhat warily, and in a subsequent photo his host, to the amusement of the assembled guests, is placing the kebob in Louis's mouth. Louis no doubt would have preferred a plate of red beans and rice, but he seems to be a good sport about the whole thing.

There are four scrapbooks that are filled with neatly arranged, carefully labeled news clippings. These were probably created by a clipping service or by someone associated with Louis's management. One of these is a stunning scrapbook that documents Louis's tour of England in 1932. Many of the British reviewers were astonished by Louis's virtuosity but others were bewildered by his exuberant stage manner. An unsigned review from the *Sunday Mail* (Glasgow) stated:

Louis's childhood friend Joe Lindsey led this band at Tony's Tavern in Chicago. The photo is autographed to Louis, and Louis wrote in the date and location.

...when he came on at the Palladium to do his show thousands cheered him to the echo. Others politely stuck their fingers in their ears and walked out. He was called a drunken bull, an untrained gorilla from some African jungle wearing a slop-tailor's ready-made suit, a human shower bath of perspiration, and an insult to music hall patrons. Through it all Armstrong grinned with the pearliest smile that ever escaped the toothpaste ads. The only thing that cuthim was that remark about his tailoring. He travels 139 suits in 48 trunks, and prides himself on the distinctive cut of his clothes.[14]

THIS PAGE Louis's Egyptian hosts presented him with a scrapbook that documented his 1965 tour of Egypt. Louis plays in front of the Sphinx. This photo of Louis, Lucille, and the Sphinx, although a staged publicity shot, successfully implies the intersection of love, time, and music.

Not Blowing Their Own Trumpets—

—they waved them in applauding a little playing exhibition by Louis Armstrong, whose band is visiting the Leeds Empire. A picture taken at a gathering of musicians to meet Louis Armstrong to-day.

BIRMINGHAM
EMPIRE

MOSS' EMPIRES LTD.
Managing Directors · · R. H. GILLESPIE, W. Evans & C. GULLIVER.
Manager · · · · · · HENRY RAYMOND

6-40 | MONDAY, SEPTEMBER 19th, 1932 AND TWICE NIGHTLY | **8-50**

FIRST TIME IN BIRMINGHAM!

JOHNNY COLLINS presents
THE SENSATIONAL **LOUIS**

ARMSTRONG

KING OF THE TRUMPET—CREATOR OF HIS OWN SONG STYLE AND HIS

NEW RHYTHM BAND

LOU **RADFORD**	JIMMY **CAMPBELL**
THE POPULAR XYLOPHONIST.	A BURDEN ON THE RATES.
BEAMS' **24** BREEZY BABES FULL OF PEP, PUNCH AND PERSONALITY.	**HENGLER** BROTHERS STRONG, SILENT MEN.
LAURIE & DANCING FOOLERY **RAYNE**	**FYNE & FURLEY** BURLESQUE COMEDIANS.

JOE PEANUTS
AND HIS SIMIAN GIGOLOS
AND BRAZILIAN MONKEY JAZZ BAND.

JAMES UPTON Ltd., General Printers, Birmingham and London.

TOP Scrapbook 6 documents Louis's 1932 tour of England. This news clipping shows that other musicians idolized Louis.

LEFT An Empire Playbill touts "The Sensational Louis Armstrong, King of the Trumpet" as the headliner. But remnants of minstrelsy are apparent with the presence on the same bill of "Joe Peanuts Simian Gigolos and his Brazilian Monkey Jazz Band."

TOP This 1926 Italian record catalog supplement featured Louis on the cover. He had made his first recordings with the Hot Five less than a year before.

RIGHT Louis samples some kabob from his Egyptian hosts.

OPPOSITE PAGE Louis never hesitated to sign an autograph.

Louis Armstrong's gold-plated Leblanc trumpet, serial number 10197.
There were five trumpets discovered inside the Armstrong House:
four Selmers and this LeBlanc. (Photo by Serge Hambourg)

TRUMPETS

Perhaps the most popular items for visitors to the Armstrong Archives are Louis's trumpets. There were five B-flat trumpets discovered inside the Armstrong House. Four of them were manufactured by Selmer and the fifth was manufactured by LeBlanc; all were manufactured in Paris, and all are gold-plated. Two of the Selmers are K-modified models — reportedly Louis's favorite model — and one is a "Balanced Action" model. These are most likely the horns that he routinely performed with on stage and in the recording studio during his final years. The fourth Selmer has gorgeous chasing around the outer bell and bell pipe, and along the bell pipe just opposite the valves is inscribed "Louis 'Satchmo' Armstrong." This trumpet was probably mostly for show, although the plating on the valve pistons does exhibit a fair amount of wear. The LeBlanc trumpet rivals the engraved Selmer in visible beauty, not because of any engraving, but because "Satchmo Louis Armstrong" appears along the bell pipe in raised white gold script matching Louis's own handwriting.

For a professional performer on a wind instrument, the selection of a mouthpiece is highly personal and somewhat idiosyncratic. Not surprisingly, Louis's collection of trumpet mouthpieces varies greatly in cup size, rim width, plating, and other critical factors. Most of the mouthpieces were custom made. Among the fourteen mouthpieces are a Parduba "Harry James model" double-cup/5-star, a custom-made Shilke marked "SATCHMO - 6 30 57," and gold plated and silver plated mouthpieces made by the legendary brass instrument technician Robert Giardinelli. Musicians still tell the story of how Louis, attempting to explain the depth and the shape of the cup he desired, led Giardinelli into a bathroom, pointed to the inside of the toilet bowl, and declared, "I want a curve just like that!"

Visitors to the Louis Armstrong Archives are enjoyably surprised to discover that the curatorial staff will usually allow visitors to hold one of Louis's trumpets. (And some visitors return home with a treasured snapshot of them holding the trumpet.) The decision to allow this practice was made after appropriate deliberation, but one of the deciding factors was that among the 5,000 photos in the Archives are several dozen photos of Louis with fans backstage and in which the fans are proudly holding Louis's trumpet. So is it appropriate to let visitors touch such priceless historical artifacts? We think Louis would approve.

Professional trumpet players who visit the Armstrong Archives are allowed to try Louis's horns. Such performers, a veritable who's who of contemporary music, have included Dizzy Gillespie, Wynton Marsalis, Doc Cheatham, Jon Faddis, Jimmie Owens, Donald Byrd, Yoshio Toyama, Irakli, Arturo Sandoval, and Randy Sandke. The horns are routinely cleaned and polished, so there is negligible danger to the finishes. (Although, regrettably, we may have already lost valuable DNA — what with today's advances in cloning, well, you never know!)

Inscribed along the bell pipe of this gold plated Selmer trumpet (K-modified model, serial number 20405) is "Louis Satchmo Armstrong."

THE SATCHMO COLLECTION.

The Louis Armstrong Archives actively seeks new material related to Louis and his legacy, and these materials are shelved and cataloged separately as the Satchmo Collection. This collection — comprising private recordings, newly discovered photographs, letters from Louis to his fans, artwork depicting Louis, newly published books and videos about Louis, souvenirs of Louis's concerts, Louis Armstrong figurines, Louis Armstrong stamps from all over the world, a copy of the FBI file on Louis,[15] Corona telephone books with Louis on the cover, Louis Armstrong coffee mugs, and a wealth of other such material purchased by or donated to the Louis Armstrong Archives — increases by 100 to 200 new acquisitions each year. Soon, its contents will out number that of the Louis Armstrong Collection.

ABOVE Engraved along the bell pipe of this trumpet is "Property of Louis Armstrong." This is the same trumpet that King George V gave to Louis, who gave it to Lymun Vunk, whose widow gave it to the Louis Armstrong Archives. (Paris, 1934)

LEFT This cover of February 21, 1949, issue of *Time* has been autographed by each member of the All-Stars. (Photo: Getty Images)

TOP LEFT Louis autographed this cornet case for a thirteen year old Randy Sandke, who would grow up to be an internationally acclaimed trumpet player.

RIGHT Commemorative cachet from the first day of issue for the Louis Armstrong stamp. (New Orleans, September 1, 1995) The first day of issue ceremony featured musical tributes by Wynton Marsalis, Al Hirt, Doc Cheatham, and Nicholas Payton.

HERE IS A SAMPLE OF SOME OF THE MORE INTERESTING ADDITIONS TO THE SATCHMO COLLECTION:

Selmer Trumpet from King George V

Perhaps the most dazzling item in the Satchmo Collection is a gold-plated Selmer trumpet given to Louis by King George V in 1933. Years later Louis gave the trumpet to Lyman Vunk, the third chair trumpeter with the Charlie Barnett Orchestra, apparently because he admired it back stage. (One can easily imagine Louis saying, "You like it, Daddy? Here, take it!") Needless to say, it was Mr. Vunk's prized possession for the rest of his life. ("This is a gold plated trumpet that the King of England gave to Louis Armstrong and Louis gave it to me.") In 1995, thanks to the efforts of Armstrong friend Jack Bradley, Dorothea Vunk (Lyman's widow) graciously donated the trumpet to the Louis Armstrong Archives.

Autographed Cornet Case

In the summer of 1963 a thirteen-year-old cornet player approached Louis, who was sitting by himself in a dressing room during intermission from a performance at the University of Chicago, and asked him to autograph his cornet case. The boy didn't have a pen, so he grabbed an eyeliner pencil from the adjacent theatre department, and Louis used it to sign the case. The young boy was Randy Sandke, who today is a jazz trumpet player of international reputation. In 2001, Sandke donated his prized case to the Armstrong Archives.

Autographed Handkerchief

Louis adored the work of Italian singer Ray Martino — he mentioned him in several published interviews and the Archives has two tapes of Louis playing along with Martino recordings. Martino, who resides in Milan, has visited the Armstrong House & Archives several times, and has given us many treasures. One of these is a white handkerchief (Louis almost always performed with one in his hand) which Louis autographed in green ink to Martino's wife: "To Sweet Lucy from Satchmo 1959".

RIGHT In this set of matryoshka (Russian nesting dolls), Louis is the biggest, followed by Miles Davis, Dizzy Gillespie, Charlie Parker, and a tiny alto saxophone.

Matryoshka Dolls

Given Louis's international celebrity, it is no surprise that the Louis Armstrong Archives has acquired not just one, but two sets of Armstrong matryoshka dolls, the nesting dolls from Russia. The first set includes five jazz greats, one inside the other. Louis is of course, the largest, outside figure. The inner figures are — from largest to smallest — Miles Davis, Dizzy Gillespie, and Charlie Parker. The second set of matryoshka dolls also contains four dolls, but each is a smiling Louis, identical except for size.

Quilt from P.S. 143.

In 1994, fifth and sixth graders at the Louis Armstrong School (P.S. 143), in Corona, Queens, made a stunning patchwork quilt depicting influential scenes from Louis's life. The project was the inspiration of Mary Ann Veidt, an avid Armstrong fan who had taught at the school for over two decades. The children, after much study, identified key places, people, or events in Louis's life and then, using an appliqué technique with felt, thread, yarn, buttons, and other notions, created twenty-five panels to depict them. Among the panels are: "What a Wonderful World" accompanied by a colorful rainbow; Louis's 1961 visit to Africa; three 78 records and a Victrola; "Skeleton in the Closet" from the film Pennies From Heaven; Arvell Shaw and Louis; Louis's House in Corona, and, in the center of the quilt, a golden trumpet with a white handkerchief. The quilt was briefly exhibited at the school and then Ms. Veidt donated it to the Armstrong Archives, where it continues to charm visitors.

TOP LEFT Marinta Skupin, Satchmo, 2002, 40.5 x 50.5 cm. This oil portrait by Marinta Skupin wonderfully captures Louis's depth and sensitivity. Peggy Alexander, our Curator, purchased it from a shop in the French Quarter of New Orleans.

TOP RIGHT When pouring from this English-made tea pot, the tea comes out of Louis's trumpet.

LEFT Students from the Louis Armstrong Elementary School (P.S. 143) in Louis's neighborhood made this quilt under the supervision of their teacher, Maryann Veidt. Each of the twenty-five panels depicts a significant event or place in Louis's life.

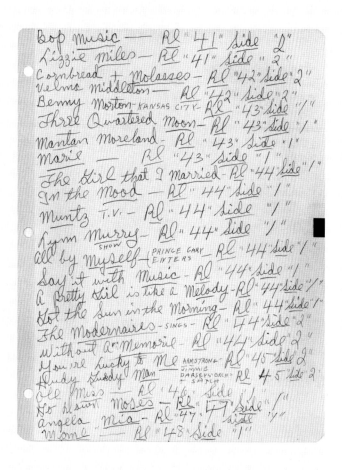

Unpublished Recordings

George Avakian's life has been intriguingly intertwined with Louis's. While still a Yale undergraduate, George was hired by Columbia Records to help with a reissue of Louis's early recordings — to his supervisor's surprise, he discovered previously unknown Hot Five recordings in the vaults. He went onto become one of the most respected and beloved producers in jazz and produced monumental LPs by Duke Ellington, Miles Davis, and Louis Armstrong (e.g., Louis Armstrong Plays W.C. Handy and Satch Plays Fats). Avakian has donated to the Archives dozens of tapes that include candid conversations with Louis, unissued broadcasts, and other one-of-a-kind treasures.

Photographs

The Satchmo Collection acquires dozens of photographs each year. Most are photos that fans took of Louis years ago, and now they wish to find a permanent home for them. But many professional photographers also donate gorgeous images. William Carter, an award-winning photographer who also heads the San Francisco Traditional Jazz Society donated a dozen handsome prints taken during Louis's performance at Cornell University in the early 1960s, jazz writer and photographer Herb Snitzer, donated photos taken during his "on the road" with Louis, and Lisl Steiner donated a candid photo of Louis relaxing in a Buenos Aires hotel room.

But not every photo we acquire is of Louis himself. People send us photos of Louis Armstrong paintings, the Place Louis Armstrong street sign in Paris (Arrondissement 13e), and other sights. In 1999 Armstrong Archives employee Deslyn Downes was visiting Grenada, her homeland, when she spotted, to her delight, a twelve-foot high Louis Armstrong puppet performing on the streets of St. George's. She grabbed a camera and snapped photos which, when she returned to New York, she added to the Satchmo Collection.

Winfried Maier Gifts

Winfried Maier first got to meet Louis while driving him to the Berlin airport — the flight was delayed and he and Louis spent the next three hours drinking beer and eating sausages. They continued to correspond and every time Louis appeared in Berlin, they would get together. Maier made his first trip to the United States in 2002 and spent an entire day at the Louis Armstrong House & Archives. He was extremely moved — in part because Louis had invited him to come to New York but Maier was never able to do so. He has continued to shower the Archives with gifts, including 8 mm films he took of Louis, many rare photos, master audio tapes of Berlin concerts, and photographs of recipients of the "Satchmo Cup," awarded to the winner of an annual wrestling tournament sponsored by Maier.

LEFT Berliner Winfried Maier and Louis Armstrong in October 1961. Maier has donated much of his extensive collection of home movies, photos, and memorabilia to the Louis Armstrong Archives.

OPPOSITE PAGE LEFT Louis created at least three catalogs of his tape collection. He typically concluded pages by writing "S'all," i.e., "That's all on this tape."

OPPOSITE PAGE RIGHT This index to Louis's tape collection is arranged by last word, e.g., "In the **Mood**," "Girl that I **Married**," etc.

THIS PAGE AND OPPOSITE PAGE
Louis's charisma is wonderfully
captured in this set of six publicity
shots. (Chicago, c. 1933)

ABOVE Performing at Fort Barrancas in Pensacola, Florida. (1941) Louis described this visit in great detail in a 14-page letter to Leonard Feather. (The letter has been published in Joshua Berrett's The Louis Armstrong Companion.)

LEFT Photos of Louis on the bandstand are plentiful, but photos of the audience are rare. Louis labeled this photo, as "Elks Ballroom, Los Angeles, Calif." (1940s)

These production stills from the motion picture *Doctor Rhythm* are rare because Louis's scene was cut from the picture. The Louis Armstrong Archives holds six production stills from the film. (1937)

1720-56

TOP Bop City (New York). Left to right: Emmett Berry (trumpet player), Lucille, Louis, and Count Basie. Emmett autographed the photo folder, "When I say it was a ball, it was a ball." (1950s)

RIGHT Louis has a twinkle in his eye as he poses backstage at Billy Berg's in Hollywood. Judging from the hairdos and the clothes, these ladies might be in show business. (September 3, 1947)

RIGHT Louis with Brooklyn Dodgers
Junior Gilliam and Don Newcomb.
Unlike most dressing room visitors,
Newcomb is holding the trumpet
correctly — perhaps he played trumpet.
(Jazz trivia: Sonny Rollins is nicknamed
"Newk" because of his resemblance to
Newcomb.)

BOTTOM Sammy Davis Jr. lights Louis's
cigarette. This photo was taken during
the filming of *A Man Called Adam,* in
which Davis portrayed a jazz trumpet
player. (1965) (Photo by Jack Bradley)

OPPOSITE PAGE TOP Louis and Jack Teagarden goof for the camera — Louis by playing flute (he's holding it backwards) and Jack by playing the trumpet (which, being a trombonist, he could probably do). (1950s)

MIDDLE & BOTTOM OPPOSITE PAGE Because Louis was so photogenic, he was often asked to pose in unusual situations. He was always a good sport about it. (Late 1950s)

TOP Louis with Xavier Cugatt and Charo. (1960s) (Photo by Bill Mark)

BOTTOM During a visit to the Berklee College of Music, Louis posed for a photo with students Arif Mardin and Toshiko Akiyoshi. Mardin would become one of the music industries most acclaimed producers and Akiyoshi would become a celebrated composer and bandleader. (c. 1956)

123

ABOVE Louis and Billie Holiday. (1950s)

TOP LEFT Clarence, Louis, Lucille, and two unidentified ladies at the New Club DeLisa which was famous for its elaborate floor shows. The V-Victory logo and the window mat date this photo in the early 1940s.

BOTTOM LEFT A candid shot at the Blue Note in Chicago. In the foreground are: Bobby Hackett (behind Lucille), Louis, Lucille, Clarence, unidentified man, Dick Cary, Peanuts Hucko, unidentified man, and Big Sid Catlett.

For years, musicians have been telling stories that when the Pope offered his hand for his ring to be kissed, Louis "gave him five" or that when the Pope asked Louis and Lucille if they had any children, Louis replied, "No, Daddy but we're still wailin'!" Those stories are disproved by these photos of Louis's audience with Pope Paul VI which show an extremely reverent Louis. (February 7, 1968)

ABOVE Photographer and musician William Carter took this photo of Louis warming-up for a performance at Cornell University. (1960s) Fans sometimes forget that every hour on the bandstand is supplemented by many hours of practicing.

TOP LEFT Songwriter Jimmy McHugh (composer of "I Can't Give You Anything But Love" and "On the Sunny Side of the Street," two of Armstrong's biggest hits) greets Louis at the Trianon Ballroom Café. He has signed it "I Can't Give You Anything but Love, Louie."

BOTTOM LEFT This photo of Nat King Cole and Louis was taken during a party to celebrate Louis and Lucille's 15th wedding anniversary. (1957)

ABOVE This is one of the only known pictures of Louis's father. He left the family when Louis was an infant and — except for when Louis briefly lived with him after leaving the Waif's Home — they had very little contact.

TOP RIGHT Lucille, Louis, Lionel Hampton, and Clarence at the New Grand Terrace Café. (1950s)

RIGHT Louis samples a new dish in Norway. He obviously would prefer to be eating red beans and rice.

BACKGROUND Louis plays tourist in Rome. (1959)

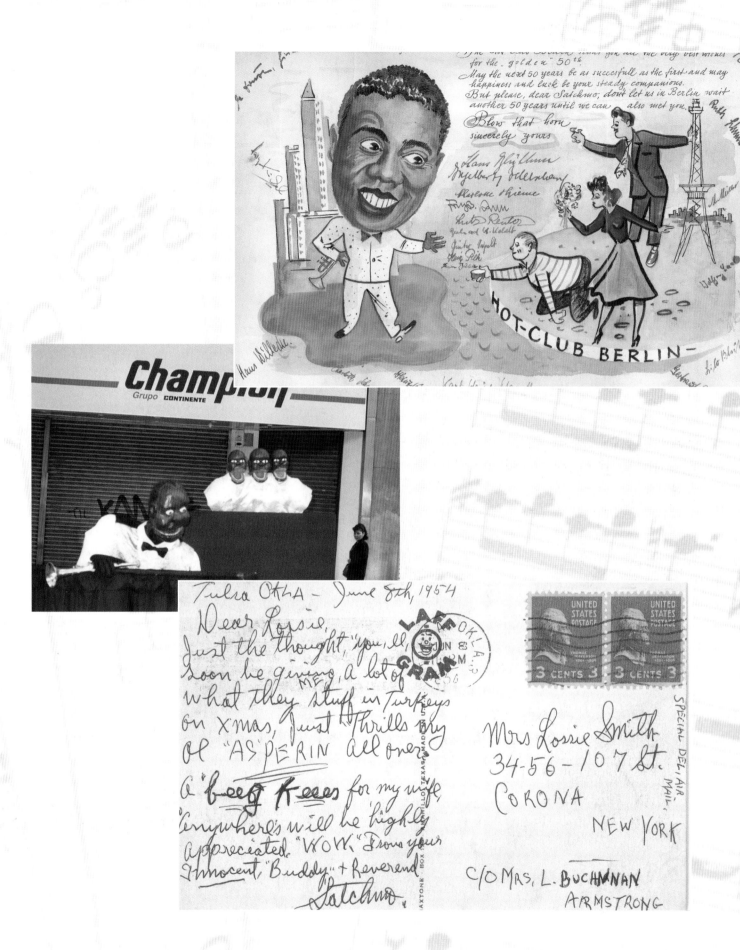

LEFT The Louis Armstrong Orchestra carried their music in cases such as this one. Apparently, after Louis broke up the orchestra in 1947, he carried the cases into his house, stuck them in a closet in the basement, where they sat for forty years. This case was used by Louis, i.e. "Leader." (Photo by Ron Eckstein)

BELOW The Archives holds 270 sets of band parts from the Louis Armstrong Orchestra. Many of them were performed but never recorded. (Photo by Ron Eckstein)

OPPOSITE PAGE TOP This hand painted certificate was given to Louis by the Hot Club of Berlin. The Archives has 120 gold records, awards, and certificates.

OPPOSITE PAGE MIDDLE In 1999 House & Archives employee Deslyn Downes spotted this Armstrong puppet on the streets of St. George's, Grenada. She purchased a disposable camera and snapped a photo for the Archives.

OPPOSITE PAGE BOTTOM Louis was a prolific correspondent who routinely sent postcards and letters to his friends and family.

LEFT Members of the Jack Hylton band greet Louis in the dressing room of the Palladium Theatre in London. (1932)

BOTTOM RIGHT Louis, Lucille, and Clarence enjoy a night out at Club Harlem in Atlantic City. (1950s)

BOTTOM LEFT Although the comic actor Nicodemus Stewart appeared with Louis in the motion picture *Cabin in the Sky* (1943), the autograph indicates that Stewart gave this photo to Louis years earlier.

[1] Within a few years, jazz masters Donald Byrd and Jimmy Heath would join the faculty. Louis Armstrong Archives, Queens College.

[2] In 1995 the Armstrong House and the Armstrong Archives, which had been separate departments at Queens College, were united and my title was changed to Director, Louis Armstrong House & Archives.

[3] One cannot help but compare Louis's collage work to the great Romare Bearden — the black American artist who is justly famous for his work in collage. Bearden began making collages in 1963.

[4] Letter from Louis Armstrong to Marli Mardon, 27 September 1953. Letter 1/12, Louis Armstrong Collection, Louis Armstrong Archives.

[5] Louis Armstrong. *Louis Armstrong: In His Own Words*, edited by Thomas Brothers. New York: Oxford University Press, 1999.

[6] Louis Armstrong, [Joke book], Manuscript 6, Louis Armstrong Collection, Louis Armstrong Archives.

[7] See especially Bill Crow, Jazz Anecdotes (New York: Oxford University Press, 1990), a wonderful anthology of musician jokes, road stories, one-liners, classic comebacks, etc.

[8] In the manuscript, Louis misspells Singleton's name as "Zootie."

[9] Richard Meryman, *Louis Armstrong — A Self Portrait* (New York: Eakins Press, 1971): 24.

[10] As "Lucifer's helpers," Louis, Willie Best, and Rex Ingram, and Mantan Moreland devise a plan to ensnare a likeable everyman named "Little Joe" — played by Eddie "Rochester" Anderson—using a winning Irish Sweepstakes ticket and the irresistible charms of "Georgia Brown" — played by a luscious Lena Horne.

[11] Scrapbook 6, Louis Armstrong Collection, Louis Armstrong Archives.

[12] Discussed in some detail in Giddins' *Satchmo* so I won't describe it here.

TOP Louis was so fond of the lip balm made by Franz Schüritz (Mannhein, Germany) that he allowed his name to be used on the product without royalties. In return, Schüritz promised to keep Louis well-supplied. Today, there are two cases of it in the Armstrong Archives.

LEFT Louis makes a Bronx cheer in front of a poster for Buck and Bubbles, the song and dance team who were his good friends.

IV Discoveries from the Armstrong Archives

Louis was a champion of the herbal laxative Swiss Kriss. He passed it out to everybody including members of the royal family of England. Swiss Kriss is sold in the gift shop of the Louis Armstrong House.

When we began to process the materials that now comprise the Louis Armstrong Collection, there was scant evidence of Louis's "original order" (the archival term for how the person who created the collection kept it arranged). The materials had been shifted and moved and boxed and re-boxed so many times between Louis's passing in 1971 and my arrival in 1991, that the lack of evidence was certainly no surprise. After study and consultation, we elected to arrange the collection by physical format — put the scrapbooks together, put the photographs together, put the reel-to-reel tapes together, etc.— and to subarrange by chronology or subject or whatever other criteria made sense for the format. The result is a fully processed collection in which materials are easily located, but for which materials relating to a specific topic (e.g., Louis's first trip to Africa) are typically scattered across various formats (e.g., photos of the African tour are in "Photos," itineraries are in "Personal Papers," African souvenirs are in "Artifacts," etc.). But by bringing together diverse materials from various formats in several collections, we can make many exciting discoveries about central relationships in Louis's life and career.

LEFT Louis's second tour of Africa was sponsored by Pepsi-Cola, which had opened new bottling plants in six African cities. This photo was used in advertisements that were circulated throughout Ghana and Nigeria. (1960)

BOTTOM LEFT Enjoying the sauna in Paris.

BELOW Louis visits with musicians in Africa. (1960)

TOP LEFT Alpha pasted into her scrapbook pairs of ticket stubs from events that she and Louis attended. She has labeled these stubs, "My Darling's" and "Mine."

TOP RIGHT The baby cries and Louis mugs along with her. (Paris, c. 1960)

LEFT Left to right: Yvone and Maurice Cullaz, Lucille, Hugues Panassie, Louis, Mezz Mezzrow, and Lily Coleman. (Paris, c. 1960)

134

WALKER HILL PHOTO SHOP
KOREA

LEFT Louis poses in a traditional Korean costume while performing at Walker Hill, an R&R resort for American servicemen. (1950s)

BELOW Writing his name on the wall, right under the names of Hugues Panassie and Madeliene Gautier (co-founders of the Hot Club of France).

Louis in Lausanne, Switzerland. (c. 1934)

LOUIS'S MARRIAGES

Louis was married four times. The exact dates of his four marriages and three divorces provide a misleading chronology because Louis had a propensity not to get a divorce from one wife until he needed it to marry the next one. A more practical chronology would detail when he was with whom. Despite the occasional overlap in marriages and relationships (i.e., being with one woman while he was still married to another), there is little doubt that Louis was passionately in love with each wife when he married her. But being married to Louis Armstrong had to have been a challenge. He was a creative genius who was willful and opinionated. He was constantly touring and performing, and his life followed a steeply ascending arc of fame and fortune. He was so genuinely unselfish with his money and his time that he belonged more to his public than to any spouse.

DAISY PARKER ARMSTRONG

When Louis met Daisy, who would become his first wife, she was a twenty-one year old prostitute in Gretna, a neighborhood in Jefferson Parish just across the Mississippi River from New Orleans. Louis, who was eighteen, was playing cornet in the house band at the Brick House, a rough and tumble honky-tonk frequented by levee workers. Drunken knife fights were common and many years later Louis recalled the Brick House as "one of the toughest joints I ever played in."[1] Daisy worked her trade at the Brick House, and Louis spotted the pretty, petite Creole woman right away. He said that, "For about three Saturday nights straight I kept noticing one of the gals looking at me with the stuff in her eyes. I kept on playing but I started giving her that righteous stuff in return. That chick was Daisy Parker."[2] After an on again - off again relationship lasting several months, they impulsively married at New Orleans City Hall, but didn't actually begin living together for another several months because they couldn't afford to set up house.

Louis and Daisy's relationship was passionate and volatile. They frequently fought and when things got too bad Louis would retreat to his mother's house. Once, while Louis was a pallbearer for a friend's funeral sponsored by the Tammany Social Aid and Pleasure Club, Daisy suddenly appeared, possessed by a jealous rage — apparently unjustified — and grasping a razor. Louis, decked out in his only suit and new patent leather shoes, fled for safety. But his new Stetson hat, for which he had saved for months, fell into the mud and Daisy grabbed it and sliced it to pieces. Daisy departed as abruptly as she had arrived and Louis, humiliated in front of friends and onlookers, completed his duties for the funeral. When he arrived home, fully expecting to make up, Daisy was waiting for him with a stockpile of bricks and began to hurl bricks at him, one by one. Neighbors summoned the police and she ended up going to jail, but Louis pulled some strings and got her paroled. Is it any wonder that, when in 1922 Louis received the telegram from King Oliver inviting him to move to Chicago and join his band, Louis left Daisy behind in New Orleans?

By far the most complete account of Louis and Daisy's marriage is contained in Louis's 1954 autobiography, *Satchmo: My Life In New Orleans*.[3] There are no archival materials relating to Daisy in the Louis Armstrong Archives. Whatever photographs or household items or other tangibles that might teach us something about Daisy disappeared long before Louis settled in Corona in 1943.

TOP RIGHT The band bus for the Louis Armstrong Orchestra. The NRA decal ("National Reconstruction Act") dates this photo in the early 1930s.

RIGHT Unloading equipment at the Corsicana Hotel. (Texas, early 1930s)

BACKGROUND Louis autographed this picture to the Belgian writer Robert Goffin, author of the Armstrong biography *Horn of Plenty*. (1932)

LILLIAN HARDIN ARMSTRONG

Louis's second wife was Lillian Hardin, who was the pianist in King Oliver's Creole Jazz Band when Louis joined the band in 1922. For Louis, Lil was everything that Daisy was not. She was college educated (Lil claimed that she was valedictorian at Fisk University but contemporary researchers have been unable to verify this), played classical and jazz piano, had common sense, was ambitious, and was frugal with money. They hid their gradually blooming romance from everyone, including the other musicians in the Creole Jazz Band, but finally tied the knot on February 5, 1924. That Louis, a former street kid from New Orleans, and the sophisticated Lil had fallen in love astounded everyone who knew them. In a manuscript discovered in the Archives, Louis recalled that, "Lillian Hardin + I finally stopped Ducking + Dodging with our secret romance and Got Married. UMP UMP UMP! There now — the whole town Gossip really started. The whole King Oliver Band, was so surprised, until they were all speechless."[4] He went on to explain that:

TOP Waiting for the band bus. (1930s)

ABOVE A musician's life is not always glamorous. Before you load the bus you must carry the carry the equipment. (Tallulah, Louisiana, early 1930s)

RIGHT Louis always owned the latest technology. (1) Louis with his movie camera during a tour of the south in the early 1930s. (2) Louis shoots a movie in Houston, Texas, in the early 1930s. Louis numbered these snapshots in green ink.

After the Lincoln Gardens⁵ let out — the first night Lil and I got married — we made the 'Rounds to all of the After Hour spots. And Everywhere we went, everybody commenced throwing a lot of Rice on us. My my — I often wondered — where on earth did they find so much Rice. Why — every place that we would leave — in front of the door was real white — the same as if there had been a real heavy snow on the ground — from so much Rice lying thrown around. Lillian and myself, we did not take a Honeymoon, or anything like that. We both thought — it would be a better idea to save all the money we could and try and buy ourselves a nice little pad (a home) — kinda lookout for a rainy day. It is — an old saying, and it has been around for Generations. Instead of a Honeymoon, we went on tour with King Oliver + his Band. We saved our money together. And, we accumulated quite a bit of Loot (money) together. And — sure enough — we really did save enough money to buy a very nice family house, in Chicago of course — at 421 East 44th Street. We were both lucky in buying this house. Because the people who had it in front of us certainly did leave it in real fine — good shape. We didn't have to do a thing but move in with our furniture.⁶

Louis and Lil's house in Chicago has the distinction of being the only home that Louis ever owned other than the Queens residence he acquired with Lucille twenty years later.

Lil served a vital role in Louis's professional evolution in that she encouraged him to leave the Creole Jazz Band, convincing him that he was destined for greater achievements than playing second cornet beside Joe Oliver and that Oliver was keeping Louis in the band in part so that Louis would not compete with him. In October 1924, Louis moved to New York City to join the great Fletcher Henderson Orchestra. He and Lil were still married and she would occasionally travel to New York to visit Louis. He returned to Chicago in November 1925 because he was unsatisfied with his role in the Henderson Orchestra — he was given relatively few chances to solo and was seldom allowed to sing — and because Lil demanded that he return to be with her — she missed him as a husband and had plans for him as a trumpet player.

Louis is resplendent in a white suit and a Panama hat upon his return to New Orleans in 1931. Alpha pasted this snapshot into her scrapbook.

TOP Louis, Zutty Singleton, and friends go swimming.

LEFT When Louis returned to New Orleans in 1931 he sponsored a baseball team called "Armstrongs Secret 9." A note on the back of the photos indicates that the team was so proud of its new uniforms that they refused to slide and lost every game. (Photo by V. Paddio)

But Lil and Louis's marriage became increasingly unhappy, perhaps because of the very differences that had first attracted them to each other. Lil often reprimanded Louis and little Clarence, who sometimes lived with them, for what seemed to be petty transgressions. Louis recalled that, "But still with all of that swell Home, Lil, and I had — There was not happiness there. We were always Fussing and threatening to 'Break up if I 'sat on the "Bed after it was made up."[7] Lil played piano on almost all the Hot Five and Hot Seven sessions (1925-1928) but was replaced by Earl Hines on the final session. By 1928 they were both involved with other people — Louis was already courting Alpha — and when Louis moved back to New York City in 1929 their marriage was essentially over.

Lil never remarried, continued to call herself "Lillian Hardin Armstrong," and maintained a successful career as a pianist, bandleader, and songwriter. Now that they were no longer living together as husband and wife, the affection that she and Louis originally felt for each other returned somewhat and in later years Lil would often attend Louis's gigs and greet him backstage. In the Archives are a more than a dozen candid photographs of Lil and Louis visiting backstage or sitting together at a nightclub table.

After Louis passed away in July 1971, Lucille was insistent that the service not be held until Lil could arrive. Lil flew to Queens and Lucille arranged for her to stay with the Armstrongs' friends and next-door neighbors, the Heraldos. On the 27th of August, Lil, back in Chicago, was performing at an outdoor memorial concert to Louis when she had a heart attack and died. Her passing seemed an eerie reminder that her life was forever linked to Louis's.

ALPHA SMITH ARMSTRONG

When Louis was performing with the Erskine Tate Orchestra at the Vendome Theatre, soon after his return to Chicago in 1925, he fell in love with a strikingly pretty, nineteen year old named Alpha Smith, who had been coming to the Vendome shows twice per week just to sit in the front row and flirt with Louis. Louis and Lil's marriage was becoming increasingly tense, and Louis was one who preferred to avoid rather than to confront domestic conflict. Alpha had a sweet nature and adored Louis in the ways that a nineteen-year-old girl adores a tremendously gifted and publicly popular musician. It was little surprise that the two became attracted to each another. That Clarence immediately took to both Alpha and her mother erased all doubts in Louis's mind that Alpha was now the gal for him.

Louis and Alpha made a striking couple. Although Louis would always be a down-home New Orleans street kid at heart, he was now a sophisticate. He had traveled up and down the Mississippi, lived in New York City, performed with the famous Fletcher Henderson Orchestra, and was a featured soloist with the Vendome Theatre Symphony Orchestra. He was a sharp dresser and a charmer. Louis had the income to buy Alpha furs and diamonds, and she looked great wearing them.

TOP The wild iconography (Louis as a cowboy, complete with chaps and a six-shooter) and text ("joyously sense the throb of its rhythm") of this Okeh Records advertisement is indicative of how jazz was marketed in the 1920s.

BOTTOM The dishes on this gag menu are named after Armstrong band members.

One of the most stunning discoveries in the Armstrong Archives is a scrapbook lovingly compiled by Alpha during her and Louis's early years together. The scrapbook itself is an 8-inch by 12-inch volume with pages made from black, heavy stock paper and is a typical of the scrapbooks so popular in that era. (But because of its acidity and fragility, today this type of scrapbook is an archivist's nightmare.) But the contents are a revelation. There's a handbill announcing the opening of the "Shady Rest" restaurant which will serve "chicken dinners, barbecue, meats, sandwiches, etc." And written at the bottom of the handbill in pencil is Alpha's annotation, "Darling and I went Sunday, May 29, 1927." (Oh, how wonderful if all scrapbook compilers were as meticulous as Alpha!) It has ads for Louis's recordings, including a splendid ad from Okeh Records for Louis's recording of "I'm a Ding Dong Daddy from Dumas" that features an illustration of Louis wearing cowboy chaps, bandanna, and pointing a six-shooter in the air. There is an official looking "Permit" which, with the two blanks for names filled in by hand, reads:

> *This is to certify that I, the legally wedded wife of Louis Armstrong do hereby permit my husband to go where he pleases, drink what he pleases and when he pleases, and I furthermore permit him to keep and enjoy the company of any lady or ladies he sees fit, as I know he is a good judge. I want him to enjoy life in this world, for he will be a long time DEAD. Signed, Mrs. A. Armstrong.*

There's a pair of elegant silhouettes cut out from black paper, one of Alpha and one of Louis, that they probably posed for and purchased while on a date. And a menu from the Ritz Café in Memphis that is offering on October 7, 1931, a "Louis Armstrong dinner" at "60 cents per Person." A 1931 handbill advertising a baseball game between Louis Armstrong's Secret Nine (a New Orleans team to which Louis donated uniforms) and the New Orleans Black Pelicans states that "Louis Armstrong will appear in person at the game and pitch the first ball."

There are dozens of newspaper clippings, including an announcement of the publication by Melrose Music of 125 Jazz Breaks for Cornet (the first collection of transcriptions of Louis's improvised solos), pieces on Louis's appearances with Floyd Campbell, Clarence Jones, Carroll Dickerson, and other groups, and an obituary for Louis's mother that begins "Mrs. Mary Armstrong, mother of

TOP A rare studio portrait of Louis and his third wife, Alpha. (1932)

MIDDLE TWO Louis and Alpha during a tour of the south. (Early 1930s)

RIGHT Louis and his buddies had this photo taken in a Coney Island shop soon after their arrival in New York (1929). Louis autographed the photo to Alpha (his third wife) but, ironically, the boat is named Lucille (the name of Louis's fourth wife, whom he would meet a decade later).

Louis Armstrong the famed jazz cornetist, died Wednesday morning at the home of her son, 421 East 44th Street, Chicago." A piece titled "Shame on Armstrong," clipped from a New Orleans paper, tells how, when Louis attended the funeral of the great cornetist Buddy Petit, so many people wanted to see him, touch, him, and even kiss him that, as the reporter somewhat sulkily observes, "unconsciously the great Louis Armstrong stole another show, and this time from a dead man." And an article with a dateline of Houston, Texas, tells how Louis performed for a crowd that "was estimated at eight thousand and was composed of representative members of both races."

In addition to news stories and advertisements, Alpha also pasted into the scrapbook sentences about Louis that she had clipped from larger articles. These provide titillating nuggets of information such as, "Louis Armstrong, ace of trumpeters, carries half a dozen mouthpieces around in his vest pocket. They range from bakelite to gold," and "Louis Armstrong, who hails from New Orleans, bears the title 'Iron Lip' in the Crescent City. Demonstrated this by playing ten choruses of 'Tiger Rag" to end on E flat above high C at the Regal last week."

There is a miniature birch bark canoe, a souvenir from the lakes region, and tied to it is a tag that on one side reads, "Oh! To be in a Canoe with you at Baldwin, Mich." and on the other is the address, "Miss Alpha Smith, 3130 Rhodes Ave., Chicago, IL, from Louis Armstrong." A two-cent stamp affixed to the tag was all that was needed for the mailman to deliver it to Alpha.

There are a dozen or more pairs of ticket stubs from events that Louis and Alpha attended together such as the Sells-Floto Circus and a White Sox baseball game and for concerts at Madison Square Garden, the Ziegfeld Theatre, and the Blackstone Theatre. Each pair of stubs is annotated in Alpha's pretty script. For their balcony seats at the Blackstone Theatre, on one ticket is "Louis (Darling)" and on the other "Mine." The tickets for ringside seats to the Malone vs. Langford boxing match are marked "Darling's seat" and "Mine" as well as "Malone won in decision."

When Louis moved back to New York City in 1929, he and the guys in the Carroll Dickerson orchestra spent weeks driving east in Model-Ts and journeyed forty miles out of their way to see Niagara Falls. Discovered in Alpha's scrapbook are snapshots that Louis and his band mates took along the way. One page has three photos of Louis and his buddies, in overcoats and touring caps, posing for the camera. The captions read, from left to right, "Having lots of fun in Niagara Falls on our way to N.Y.," "In Canada on way to N.Y.," and "In New York." One of several snapshots of the falls itself bears Louis's writing, "Niagara Falls" and "See the boat in the center?" (referring to the Maid of the Mist). Among the other candid snapshots in the scrapbook is one of Louis and friends swimming in a lake, probably before their departure from Chicago.

PERMIT

This is to certify that I, the legally wedded wife of _Louis Armstrong_ do hereby permit my husband to go where he pleases, drink what he pleases and when he pleases, and I futhermore permit him to keep and enjoy the company of any lady or ladies he sees fit, as I know he is a good judge. I want him to enjoy life in this world, for he will be a long time DEAD.

Signed _Mrs. A. Armstrong_

LEFT Alpha probably bestowed this gag permit upon a much-amused Louis.

BOTTOM LEFT Louis's triumphal return to New Orleans in 1931 was observed in many ways, including this baseball game held on "Louis Armstrong Day."

BELOW Alpha lovingly annotated this menu, "Darling and I went Sunday, May 29, 1927," and then pasted it into her scrapbook.

LOUIS ARMSTRONG DAY !

BASE-BALL

"King" of the Trumpet

PRESENTS

Armstrong Secret Nine
IN A GAME VS.
N. O. BLACK PELICANS
WINNER TO PLAY
Galveston Sand Crabs
HEINEMANN PARK
DOUBLE HEADER
Sunday, August 16th
Also MONDAY, AUGUST 17th

LOUIS ARMSTRONG will appear in person at the game and pitch the first ball with Mike McKendricks on the receiving end Sunday will be Louis Armstrong Day in New Orleans, look for advertisement, Sunday, August 16th from 11 to 1 P. M.
FIRST GAME STARTS AT 2 P. M.

50c GENERAL ADMISSION 50c

SPECIAL ACCOMMODATIONS FOR WHITE PATRONS

Franklin 0351 WILLIAM'S PRINTING SERVICE 930 N. Clabiorne Ave.

ANNOUNCING THE OPENING

of

Shady Rest

Saturday, May 28, 1927

135 Claire Boulevard
ROBBINS, ILL.

W. C. BISHOP, Proprietor.

CHICKEN DINNERS,
BARBECUE, MEATS,
SANDWICHES, Etc.

One mile West of Blue Island—South-Western Avenue to Broadway, Blue Island, turn left at 135 Claire Street.

THIS PAGE When Louis and the guys in the Carroll Dickerson band moved to New York in 1929, they drove forty miles out of their way to see Niagara Falls. Louis sent Alpha these annotated snapshots which she pasted into a scrapbook.

(Right) "Having lots of fun in Niagara Falls on our way to New York."

(Middle) Louis wrote on the snapshot of Niagara Falls, "See down here?" The birch bark canoe is a souvenir from Baldwin, Michigan, which he mailed to her using a two-cent stamp.

(Bottom) "In Canada on way to New York."

(Background) "In New York."

While at Coney Island Louis and his buddies had their picture taken in a photographer's prop rowboat, and he mailed it back to his sweetheart autographed, "To Alpha from Louis." Ironically, the boat's name, prominently painted on its bow and printed on its life preserver, is "Lucille," the name of Louis's next wife.

In 1932 Louis and Alpha sailed for Europe on the S.S. Majestic. An ocean voyage with black tie dinners and passengers on the social register was probably quite a thrill for Alpha, who not too long before had been the hired help for a white family in Chicago. (Her scrapbook, in addition to containing ticket stubs for concerts and shows, has many Pullman stubs and luggage checks — traveling was obviously exciting for Alpha.) Snapshots discovered in Louis's collection of photographs show a radiant Alpha — snappily dressed in a beret and fashionable wool skirt — and Louis relaxing on deck, posing with friends, and enjoying the sea breeze.

Louis played sold out shows in London, Denmark, and Paris and he appeared in a Danish film recorded on a Copenhagen sound stage. His European fans were thrilled to have him and he was feted with celebratory suppers and gifts. A series of photos taken at a reception in Sweden show Alpha, beautifully attired in a boldly striped dress and a brimmed hat worn at a rakish angle, and Louis, wearing a double-breasted tweed suit and spats, being warmly welcomed by their Swedish hosts.

When Louis was in Paris in 1934, Alpha was with him all of the time. A gorgeous studio portrait taken in London a year or so earlier shows Alpha and Louis, side by side, their heads gently touching. They seem to be content and comfortable with each other, but missing in this photograph is the sparkling smile that Alpha so often flashed for earlier photos (which can be explained by the formality of the studio setting or the instructions of the photographer or any other number of reasons). The photo displays a double autograph to Robert Goffin, the Belgian writer who authored a biography of Louis and who no doubt showed them around Paris. On Alpha's white collar Louis has written, "Best wishes to our Best Friend, Robert Goffin, from Louis and Alpha, 8/9/34." (The appellation "Our Best Friend" was probably sincere at the moment but overly generous.) On Louis's collar is the signature, "Alpha."

BELOW Louis and General, the Boston Terrier given to him by Joe Glaser. (1960s)

Louis and Alpha finally married on October 11, 1938. Perhaps because Louis had been married twice before, he was hesitant about getting married again. As was his way, even though he and Lil had not been together in years, he finalized his divorce on September 30th 1938, just in time to marry Alpha.

Curiously, Louis and Alpha's marriage would last only a few years. By 1940 he was involved with Lucille and by 1942 he was married to her. What happened? A splendidly detailed letter to jazz critic Leonard Feather in 1941 (fourteen-page, single-spaced, typed — a long letter even by Louis's standards) describes how Alpha has a routine for dealing with dirty laundry on the road, mentions that a newly made friend was "enjoying every moment with me and Alpha," and gives no hint of any problem between the two[8]. Gary Giddins reported that "Alpha turned out to be interested primarily in 'furs and diamonds' — 'a no good bitch,' in Armstrong's final estimation."[9] Perhaps, once the chase was over and the two were legally married, Alpha emerged as a gold digger. According to Ernie Anderson, she "shocked Louis to the quick by running off with the white drummer, Cliff Leeman."[10] We may never know for sure what caused their marriage to weaken. But Louis's reaction to the end of their marriage survives today in a song that he wrote in the 1940s, soon after he was became involved with Lucille.[11] He woke up in the middle of the night, grabbed some paper, and sat down at the hotel room desk to scribble out the words and music to a song that, a few minutes before, he had been hearing in a dream. For Louis, who had written more than fifty compositions in the early decades of his career, this would be his only composition after 1940. He titled the song "Someday, You'll be Sorry" and the lyrics are unambiguous:

> *Someday you'll be sorry*
> *The way you treated me was wrong*
> *I was the one who taught you all you know*
> *And your friends had you to make me sing another song*
>
> *So good luck may be with you*
> *and may your future, you won't fear, dear*
> *there won't be another*
> *to treat you like a brother*
> *Someday you'll be sorry dear.*[12]

Louis and Lucille's wedding. Left to right: Reverend Nance, Mrs. Nance, Lucille's mother, Lucile, Louis.

Louis and Lucille, perhaps in the Commodore record shop. Terrific hat! (1940s)

LUCILLE WILSON ARMSTRONG

After three marriages that for varied reasons didn't last, Louis finally found the right woman with Lucille. She was beautiful, talented, and well equipped to assume the quite public role of "Mrs. Louis Armstrong." But most significantly, she gave Louis a home.

Lucille and Louis first met at the Cotton Club where he was performing and she was a chorus girl. The date has been cited in some books as 1938, but it may have been as late as 1941. Louis was immediately attracted to her. As he recalled in the *Ebony* article, "Why I Like Dark Women," "When I first saw her the glow of her deep-brown skin got me deep down. When we first met, she was dancing in the line at the old Cotton Club and was the darkest girl in the line. Dark, that is, by the prevailing standards of Negro beauty. Lucille was the first girl to crack the high yellow color standard used to pick girls for the famous Cotton Club chorus line. I think she was a distinguished pioneer. I suppose I'm partial to brown and dark-skinned women anyhow. None of my four wives was a light-colored woman."[13] (This last sentence is almost certainly an editorial enhancement — the Ebony article was heavily edited — because Daisy, who was a Creole, was probably light skinned.) Louis soon discovered that Lucille was just as beautiful on the inside. As the two grew closer together he suggested marriage, and the young chorus girl was understandably apprehensive. Louis recalled their conversation:

You're Just the Gal for me. Now I know you're going to tell me that, you might be a little too young for me' since there is a difference in our ages. I am only (26) years old, she said — And you (meaning me) are around (40 or 41) somewhere around there. And I'm wondering if it would turn out O.K. Being married to a man with so much Experience behind him (3-x-wives). After all I'm just a little small Chorus Girl, Lucky to come in contact with a Bunch of Lovely Well Hipped People.[14]

But Louis had a ready response and their relationship soon jumped to another level:

That's when I stopped her from Talking by slowly reaching for her Cute little Beautifully Manicured hand and said to her, Can you Cook' Red Beans and Rice? Which amused her very much. Then it dawned on her that I was very serious. She — being a Northern girl born in N.Y. and Me, a Southern boy from N.O. She could see why I asked her that question. So She said: I've never cooked that kind of food before. But — Just give me a little time and I think that I can fix it for you. That's All that I wanted to hear, and right away I said' How about Inviting me out to your house for dinner tomorrow night? She said, Wait a minute, give me time to get it together, or my wits together, or Sompthing. We'll say a Couple of days from now? Gladly I Accepted.[15]

Then the auspicious day arrived when Louis got to sample Lucille's newly acquired recipe for red beans and rice and to meet his future in-laws. Perhaps more significantly, although Louis doesn't address the issue, Lucille's family had its first opportunity to evaluate the marriage of their precious Lucille to a world-famous musician who was constantly on tour, had already married three times before, but had — as of this dinner — only been divorced twice.

Two days later I was at their house on time with Bells on. Also my best Suit. I met her Mother Mrs. Maude Wilson. Then later I met Jackie, Janet and Sonny. They all impressed me right away as the kind of Relatives that I could be at ease being around for the rest of my life. The Red Beans + Rice that Lucille Cooked for me was just what the Doctor ordered. Very much delicious and I ate Just like a dog. I said forgive me after I had finished eating. I Just had to make some kind of excuse. She accepted it very cheerful. Because I am sure that Lucille has never witnessed any one Human Being eating So much. Especially at one Sitting. I had her to save the rest of the Beans that was left over. Then I'll come another time and finish them. We commenced getting closer "n" closer as time went by.[16]

LEFT This studio portrait from the 1950s shows a poised, confident woman.

BOTTOM LEFT "You may kiss the Bride." (October 12, 1942)

BOTTOM RIGHT A demure Lucille in England while a member of the Blackbirds of 1936.

OPPOSITE PAGE When did Louis find the time to write? This photo provides an answer. Louis is typing a letter or a manuscript in the kitchen of the Band Box, a nightclub in Chicago. Note the bell of his trumpet, the extra pair of two-tone shoes, and the five gallons of olives. (Early 1940s)

LEFT Blackbirds of 1936. Lucille is in the front row on the left.

BELOW Fifteen-year old Lucille's beauty is unmistakable in this school photo. (She is seated front row, center.) (1929)

Lucille overcame what reservations she may have held and the two fell madly in love. In the fall of 1942, while in Chicago with his orchestra for a gig, Louis appeared before a judge to get a divorce from Alpha. Louis was apprehensive during his morning appearance in court — he had been up all night partying and there was no guarantee that the judge would grant the divorce — but as the proceedings began he looked around the courtroom and saw, to his surprise and delight, Lucille, who had traveled from New York City to be with him. The divorce was easily granted — the judge knew who Louis was and was charmed by him — and Louis and Lucille then realized that they did not wish to wait any longer to get married. The next stop on the band's tour was St. Louis. Velma Middleton, the band's vocalist, was from St. Louis and offered to host the wedding in her mother's home. That suited Louis and Lucille just fine and on October 12, 1943, the two were married. Members of the band were guests and Lawrence Lucie, the guitar player, served as best man.

It was Lucille's idea to own a house and she found the house in Corona, purchased it, and decorated it without Louis ever having seen it. Their life in the house was cheerful and content, although not without the conflicts that are inevitable in any long-term relationship. All successful marriages — no matter how passionate they are, and Louis and Lucille, according to Louis's manuscripts, enjoyed an active sex life their entire marriage — require nurturing domesticity. In his later years, Louis began to sense that Lucille shared characteristics of his mother, whom he idolized:

> The more we wedged in together which's gotten better each time, I commenced to calling Ol Lucille Moms. My Moms. She's so Attentive, And she reminds me and does a lot of things just like my mother, May Ann. And since she passed in 1927, it seems as if Lucille has close features just like May Ann — Some of Lucille's ways and little gestures are just like my mother. Unconsciously it happen. Lucille — not knowing anything about it until I told her about it. And then she did feel proud.[17]

The Louis Armstrong Collection is, as would be expected, especially rich in materials about Lucille. There are at least two hundred photographs, six scrapbooks, and several cubic feet of personal papers that are solely Lucille's and have nothing to do with Louis. Many of the photos are snapshots of friends at the beach, family birthday parties, and other special occasions. But there are some wonderful photos of Lucille in her pre-Louis days. A formal portrait of a class of thirty schoolgirls in uniform shows Lucille seated in the exact center of the front row. Even as a teenager, her beauty set her apart from her classmates. Seven years later, she was a professional dancer and traveled to England as a member of the Blackbirds of 1936. A photo of her in England shows a sweet looking, sensibly dressed young lady demurely holding her purse in front of her. In a photo of her onstage, Lucille is part of a six-member dance troupe elaborately costumed in silken fall-away skirts and feathered headdresses. Lucille was very close to her mother and many of her photos in the Armstrong Archives are autographed to her mother.

After she married Louis, Lucille was frequently photographed with him at public appearances and on international tours. But several times she entered the photographer's studio to have formal portraits made. One such photo from the late 1950s or early 1960s shows a handsome, self-assured woman, with the latest hairdo and beautifully manicured nails, confidently holding a lit cigarette. Curiously, hidden just inside the folds of her blouse can be spotted a Star of David which she is wearing on a delicate chain. Louis proudly and publicly wore a Star of David because his manger Joe Glaser had given it to him as a gift and because of his affectionate remembrance of the Karnofsky family who had done so much for him when he was a child. But Lucille was a devout Catholic — perhaps the Star of David that she is wearing matches Louis's.

After a Dee'licious Meal in Prague. 1965

yum yum

TOP Louis finishes a "Deelicious Meal" while Lucille tidies up. (Prague, 1965)

RIGHT Louis and Lucille pose with their hosts during a European tour. (1960s)

OPPOSITE PAGE Louis and Lucille play miniature ice hockey with Kwame Nkrumah, the first Prime Minister of Ghana. During Louis's 1956 tour of Africa, Louis and Nkrumah posed for many formal photographs. This photo is rare because it captures a quite candid moment.

LOUIS AND CLARENCE

If any relationship in Louis's life exemplified his genuine goodness and compassion, it was his relationship with Clarence Armstrong. When Louis was an adolescent in New Orleans, two of his cousins, the sisters Sarah Ann and Flora Miles, lived nearby. Sarah Ann was closer in age to Mayann (Louis's mother) than to Louis, but Flora was Louis's age or a perhaps a year or two younger. During the spring of 1915, Flora, an unwed teenager, became pregnant. On August 8th, a severe hurricane with winds of 140 miles per hour struck New Orleans, and Louis was caught outside in it. He recalled that, "When I finally reached home I was soaking wet and exhausted. Mayann and Sarah Ann were scared to death for fear I might have been killed in the storm. I had been real frantic while I was struggling to get home for fear the wind had blown my house and family off into some strange neighborhood. When I came in I threw my arms around mother and Sarah Ann, and while I was hugging them I looked at our only bed...There I saw the baby Clarence and it took all the gloom out of me."[18]

Young Flora had suffered through a difficult delivery, the Armstrongs had no money for a doctor, and the Charity Hospital was overflowing with casualties from the storm. (Hundreds of New Orleans residents died from the hurricane.) Flora, with insight of what was to come, asked Louis to look after Clarence if anything happened to her. Mayann and Sarah Ann nursed her as best as they could, but their efforts failed and Flora died.

Louis, only fourteen years old himself, was the sole breadwinner for the household. At this time he was selling newspapers and playing cornet on whatever pick-up gigs would come his way. When times got too hard, he would gather spoiled food from garbage piles and then he and Mayann would cut out the rotten portions, dress and boil what remained, and sell baskets of the salvaged provisions to restaurants. But Louis was crazy about little Clarence and, when he wasn't out making ends meet, he would play with him for hours.

OPPOSITE PAGE Eating spaghetti
at the New Club DeLisa. Left to right:
Doc Pugh, unidentified, unidentified,
Lil Hardin, Louis, Clarence. (Early 1940s)

THIS PAGE Clarence helps Louis
celebrate his birthday. (1950s)

Louis took his promise to Flora seriously and always referred to Clarence as his adopted son. When Louis married Daisy, Clarence came to live with them. One rainy afternoon, while Louis and Daisy were listening to records, Clarence, about three or four years old at this time, was playing on the back porch. He slipped off the wet porch — which was on the second story of the building — and fell all the way to the ground. The impact apparently injured his brain and caused a life long developmental disability, or, as Louis described it, "That fall hindered Clarence all through his life. I had some of the best doctors anyone could get examine him, and they all agreed that the fall had made him feeble minded."[19] Clarence had always been a sweet child but his disability seemed to endear him to Louis even more. Louis took great care to "teach him the necessary things in life, such as being courteous, having respect for other people, and last but not least, having good common sense."[20]

After Louis became established in Chicago and married Lil, he sent for Clarence, who, with a nametag pinned to his clothes, traveled to Chicago by train. Clarence had his own room in their house and went to a special school. But the strains in Louis and Lil's marriage ("...put on airs with a certain 'Spoon for this and a certain 'fork for that"[21]) affected Clarence too, and when Clarence first visited Alpha and her mother, he immediately took to the down-home, relaxed atmosphere. After finishing off a big plate of fried chicken, Clarence exclaimed, "Pops this is where I should be living instead of staying out there with Lil.[22]" A few weeks later, Louis and Clarence moved out of the house with Lil and moved in with Alpha and her mother and stepfather.

In the 1930s, Louis evolved professionally from star to superstar, and the remaining decades of his life were characterized by almost incessant travel. But no matter how busy he became or how famous he grew, he always saw to it that Clarence had a place to live, clothes, pocket money, and even companionship. Clarence never resided with Lucille and Louis in their Corona home — some have reported that Lucille was embarrassed by Clarence's disability and disapproved of his uncultured ways — but he lived in the Bronx and socialized with Louis and Lucille frequently.

To my knowledge, only two photographs of Clarence have ever been published. One captures a 1935 party to honor Duke Ellington; there are twenty-four people in the photo and Clarence is partially hidden behind others. The second is a somewhat grainy

This photo beautifully captures Clarence's and Louis's pride and affection for each other. Louis always saw to it that Clarence had everything he needed. (Band Box nightclub, Chicago, early 1940s)

1926 photo of Louis, a teenage Clarence, and an unidentified gentleman and boy.[23] But present in the Louis Armstrong Archives are dozens of marvelous photos of Clarence. One of the finest of these was taken at the Band Box, a nightclub at 56 West Randolph Street in Chicago that was existed for only a few years in the early 1940s. The photo was taken back in the club's storeroom and in the background one can see wooden shelves stocked with boxes of replacement light bulbs. Clarence stands squarely facing the camera and Louis is to his right. Both are impeccably dressed in double-breasted suits with wide lapels and both sport folded handkerchiefs in their breast pockets. But the most striking aspect of the photo is the smiles. Louis's pride and affection for Clarence is unmistakable, and Clarence's mutual pride and contentment to be standing next to his "Pops" is also without question.

A pair of photos from the New Club DeLisa, the famous Chicago nightclub that was a major venue for black performers, captures Louis and Clarence enjoying a night on the town in the early 1940s. In one of the photos, seated around a café table are Clarence, Louis, a beaming Lucille (they were either just married or just about to be married), and two attractive women (the one in the white dress appears in several other Chicago photos — she must be a friend or relative). It's obviously an enjoyable night out for Louis and his guests, and Clarence, although he is the only one not smiling, seems happy and relaxed. The second photo shows Doc Pugh (Louis's long-time valet), two unidentified men (both of whom look like they could be in show business), Lil Hardin Armstrong, Louis, and Clarence, seated around a table filled with plates, glasses, and silverware. Louis and Clarence, each in the middle of slurping a huge forkful of spaghetti, look directly at the camera, the two unidentified men mug for the camera, and Doc Pugh and Lil gently smile at everyone else's antics. The photos are a wonderful document of Louis and Clarence's relationship, as well as proof that Lil and Louis were able, by the 1940s, to be friends once again.

Clarence appears in many other nightclub photos. He was apparently often invited along when the Armstrongs went out for the evening. A photo from the New Grand Terrance Café in Chicago shows Lucille, Louis, and Clarence seated at a table, with master drummer and vibraphonist Lionel Hampton standing beside them. Because all of the other tables visible in the background are empty, the photo must have been posed before or after a performance. But the four look fresh and alert; so chances are it is more likely 7 p.m. than 3 a.m. The outing no doubt brought back many exciting memories for Louis and Clarence because the New Grand Terrace Café occupied the site of the former Sunset Café where twenty years earlier Louis performed with the Carroll Dickerson band and where Louis later led his own band, the Sunset Stompers. (And where Louis first met Joe Glaser, his long-time manager.)

Clarence spent his final years living in a nursing home in the Bronx. Few Armstrong fans realized that Clarence was still alive[24] and Clarence's only regular visitor was Glenn Clendening, a relative of Clarence's late wife. On August 27, 1998, Clarence passed away. A group of Armstrong fans, learning that there was not enough money for a funeral and that Clarence was slated to be buried in an unmarked grace in a potter's field, pooled their money together and scheduled a simple service at a nearby funeral home. Clarence was buried in Forest Green Cemetery in Morganville, New Jersey.

LOUIS'S MANAGERS BEFORE GLASER

To appreciate why Louis and Joe Glaser reconnected in 1935 and became life-long business partners, one has to understand Louis's dilemmas with his previous managers. All of his managerial predicaments were rooted in an era of Prohibition, gin mills, speakeasies, and gangland control of nightclubs and the recording industry.

Louis returned to New York in 1929 on the invitation of Tommy Rockwell, a former recording director of Okeh Records who was ambitiously expanding his career into artist management. On May 18, 1929, Louis signed a contract to be managed by Rockwell, and soon Louis was performing in the hit Broadway show "Hot Chocolates" and cut a best selling recording of "Ain't Misbehavin'." In 1930, Rockwell had Louis in California performing at Frank Sebastian's Cotton Club in Culver City and making recordings with Jimmie Rodgers ("the Father of Country Music") and the Les Hite Orchestra (which featured a young Lionel Hampton). But during an intermission at the Cotton Club gig, Louis and drummer Vic Berton got busted for smoking marijuana. On one of his home-recorded tapes Louis explains that the bust was arranged by a rival nightclub owner who was jealous of the crowds that Armstrong was drawing. They spent a night in jail and the next morning the judge pronounced a sentence of six months in jail and a thousand dollars fine. Rockwell immediately sent an unsavory associate named Johnny Collins out to California to fix everything, which he promptly did. But Rockwell didn't anticipate that Collins would double-cross him by falsely informing Louis that he, i.e. Collins, was now his manager. Louis, not knowing any better, began to work for Johnny Collins. The situation was bound to reach a dramatic conclusion, and sure enough, it did. In April 1931 while Louis was working at the Showboat Cabaret, an Al Capone-controlled speakeasy in Chicago's loop, five gangsters approached Collins and demanded $6,000 as partial payment for stealing Louis's services; Collins had them arrested for extortion. A few days later, two more gangsters, one of whom was the notorious Frankie Foster, cornered Louis in his dressing room and demanded that he catch the next train to New York to perform at Connie's Inn. (Connie's Inn was a famous Harlem[25] nightclub owned by Connie and George Immerman.) Louis, after first feigning ignorance ("Why — that's news to me. Mr. Collins didn't tell me anything about it."[26]) soon realized that he was outmatched. They held a pistol to Louis and forced him into a telephone booth. Louis recalled that "Sooo we went to the phone (with a gun in my side) and sure enough, someone said hello, a familiar voice too — yes sir — I know that voice if I heard it a Hundred years from now. The first words he said to me was — "When are you going to open here?" I tuned and looked 'direct into Frankie Foster's face and said "Tomorrow AM."[27]

LEFT Louis and his manager Johnny Collins. Collins turned out to be an unsavory character.

BOTTOM RIGHT A 1934 program for the European concerts promoted by N. J. Canetti.

BOTTOM LEFT Collins, Louis, and Alpha in England. Louis has labeled this photo, "Entering the Ace of Spades Road House, England, 4/8/32." Oddly, in almost every photo of Collins and Louis held by the Louis Armstrong Archives, Collins is touching Louis.

LEFT A rare photo of Louis directing the French back-up band contracted by his manager N.J. Canetti. Louis has scrawled on the photo above the band, "Paris, France, 1934."

BELOW One of Louis's scrapbooks has this extremely rare photo of Louis on stage at London's Trocadero. (1932)

Louis didn't open at Connie's Inn. Louis, Collins, and the band fled Chicago and during the next six months Louis played a hastily booked series of engagements in West Virginia, Texas, Tennessee, Oklahoma, New Orleans, and almost anywhere else that wasn't New York City or Chicago. Rockwell then attempted to pressure Louis through legal means. He notified the American Federation of Musicians that Louis was violating his contract by refusing to appear at Connie's Inn. Louis — or, more accurately, attorneys hired by Collins — responded by suing Rockwell, for preventing Louis from "engaging in his lawful business and occupation,"[28] i.e., playing music. In the fall of 1931 Louis's suit went to trial in the United States District Court in Manhattan.

In 1996 the Louis Armstrong Archives acquired from the United States District Court photocopies of the entire court docket for the lawsuit of Armstrong vs. Rockwell. The files, which include affidavits, testimony of witnesses, motions, subpoenas, and exhibits, reveal a cornucopia of previously unknown facts about the complicated interaction between Rockwell and Louis in 1931. For example, jazz historians have long speculated who was on the other end of the telephone when Armstrong was with Frankie Foster — Armstrong intentionally didn't reveal the name in his manuscript quoted above which was written in the mid-1940s — but the court documents reveal that the voice who said, "When are you going to open here?" was, not surprisingly, Connie Immerman himself. The deteriorating relationship between Louis and the American Federation of Musicians is also a revelation. After Joseph Weber, president of the musician's union, telegrammed Louis to inform him that he was violating a contract to appear at Connie's Inn, Louis (more likely his attorney, hired by Collins) immediately fired off a reply:

CHICAGO. ILL, MAY 14, 1931
JOSEPH WEBER, PRESIDENT
AMERICAN FEDERATION OF MUSICIANS,
NEW YORK CITY.

ALLEGED CONTRACT AUTHORIZING ROCKWELL TO REPRESENT AND ACT FOR ME CANCELLED BY ME SEPTEMBER NINETEEN HUNDRED THIRTY. HE HAS NO AUTHORITY TO ACT FOR ME AND I PERSONALLY MADE NO AGREEMENT TO APPEAR AT CONNIE'S AT ANY TIME. ROCKWELL USING IMPROPER METHODS TO EMBARRASS ME. STOP. I HAVE NEVER VIOLATED ANY AGREEMENT MADE BY ME. STOP. CAN SUBSTANTIATE MY POSITION FULLY AND WILL BE GLAD TO SUBMIT FULL PROOF OF THE FAIRNESS AND HONESTY OF MY CONDUCT AT ALL TIMES.

LOUIS ARMSTRONG[29]

Rockwell produced a contract for Louis's engagement at Connie's Inn that was dated July 25, 1930, and therefore argued that because this contract predated Louis's cancellation of their managerial agreement, Louis was still obligated to fulfill the booking. Louis's attorneys produced handwriting experts who held that the contract could not have been signed in July and was actually signed quite recently. Weber, who for whatever reason firmly sided with Rockwell, sent Louis a series of increasingly threatening telegrams, and finally sent this one:

> 1931 JUN 4 PM 6 22
> CU351 33-HP CHATANOOGA TENN 4 558P
> LOUIS ARMSTRONG
>
> 431 EAST 44TH STREET
>
> YOU HAVE BEEN EXPELLED BY THE INTERNATIONAL EXECUTIVE BOARD FOR FAILURE TO OBEY THE FEDERATIONS ORDER STOP I AM NOTIFYING LOCALS TWO HUNDRED EIGHT AND EIGHT HUNDRED TWO ERASE YOUR NAME FROM MEMBERSHIP –
>
> JOE N WEBER[30]

Because Louis continued to perform, either the local musicians unions never expelled him or he was quickly reinstated. Weber and other union officers were eventually dropped as defendants in Louis's suit but Rockwell and Connie and George Immerman remained. Decades later the American Federation of Musicians would redeem itself by bestowing awards and recognition upon Louis.

Rockwell solicited affidavits from Paul Whiteman, Jack Kapp, and other leading figures in the world of entertainment testifying to Louis's uniqueness as a musician. The legal strategy was to demonstrate that no one could possibly substitute for Louis at the Connie's Inn engagement. Collins and Louis then turned the tables by presenting these affidavits in advertisements as glowing endorsements of Louis. Scrapbook 5 in the Archives includes several of the affidavits — inexplicably, all are typed on the stationery of the Greystone Ballroom in Cincinnati, Ohio.

For all of the abundance of information in the U.S. District Court file, the most critical piece of paper — the judge's final ruling — is curiously and frustratingly missing. News clippings imply that the judge ruled in Louis's favor. But the resolution itself was not especially significant because Louis had brought the suit solely to counterattack Rockwell and the trial had therefore served its purpose. But one thing was certain: Louis now had powerful enemies in Tommy Rockwell and Joe Weber. In July 1932, Louis and Collins sailed for England on the S.S. Majestic.

OPPOSITE PAGE Louis shares his hotel mealtime with two young reporters. (Europe, 1960s)

Louis's tour of England, although a hit with audiences, suffered from a host of logistical problems. Collins had told their English hosts that the Majestic was docking at Southampton at midday but it actually docked at Plymouth late in the evening. Collins had neglected to arrange for a hotel, and securing accommodations for black travelers in the wee hours of the morning proved almost impossible. In general Collin's professional incompetence — as well as his drunken, loutish behavior — was becoming intolerable. Louis and Collins returned to the United States in October, and Louis performed engagements in Philadelphia, Washington D.C., Illinois, Kentucky, and Indiana.

The next summer, Louis and Collins again sailed to England, this time aboard the S.S. Homeric. One evening during the sea voyage, Collins became sloppy drunk, began to berate Louis about his planned musical program, and called Louis a "nigger" in front of the entire table of diners. Collins and Louis had reached their limits, and within weeks of landing in England Louis fired Collins.

The Archives holds many snapshots of Collins and Louis together, including ones taken during the sea voyage to Europe. Collins, with a beer gut, cigar in hand, and a steely-eyed stare, looks just like the disagreeable character he proved to be. Curiously, in almost every snapshot Collins is touching Louis, e.g., a hand on the elbow or an arm around him.

In 1933 Jack Hylton, England's most popular bandleader who eight years earlier had founded a booking agency, organized several tours throughout England for Louis. Louis was backed during the tours by local groups, but these pick-up musicians were far below the caliber required, and eventually Hylton assembled a permanent back-up band which included several black expatriates, most notably saxophonist Fletcher Allen. Hylton scheduled a concert in London that would pair Louis Armstrong and the great tenor saxophonist Coleman Hawkins (the two had played together a decade earlier in the Fletcher Henderson Orchestra) and began to heavily promote the concert in The Melody Maker. But the sold-out concert was cancelled at the last minute because Louis refused to perform. Music critic Hugues Panassié later defended Louis by explaining that Louis had pulled out because Hawkins had skipped rehearsals and was generally unprepared for the high profile show.[31] But on a home-recorded tape, Louis explains that:

> *Now the incident concerning Coleman Hawkins and I during a concert in London at the time we were blowing there. Everyone should remember why the concert didn't come off. Here's why...Hawkins was with Jack Hylton- a big man from New York. So was I from New York. So Hawk didn't think I was big enough to share a concert-or top billing equal with me and some funky shit. So he and his handlers, whoever they were, they did nothing more than mention the concert and that was all that happened to that shit. I ran across Hawkins in New York and we were so glad to see each other we didn't mention England at all. Dig that shit. So you see, it was all bull-shit at the start.[32]*

The cancelled concert and the ensuing rotten publicity ended the relationship between Louis with the well meaning but beleaguered Hylton.

For much of 1934, Louis lived in Paris. While there, perhaps because he immediately realized that he would require a French-speaking manager if he were to work, he impulsively signed a contract with N.J. Canetti, an ambitious French promoter of dubious reputation. Canetti booked Louis into a concert at the Salle Pleyel and organized tours to France, Belgium, Italy, and Switzerland. He produced a handsome, 32-page concert program, "N.J. Canetti présente Louis Armstrong," filled with photographs, a biography of Louis, a listing of Louis's major recordings, and an essay by Robert Goffin about jazz spots in Harlem.[33] Canetti billed himself on the program as "Représentant exclusif de Louis Armstrong pour le Monde Entier," i.e., Louis Armstrong's Exclusive World-wide Agent." But Canetti and Louis soon had a falling-out. Louis seriously damaged his lip and then couldn't honor the tour. The higher a trumpeter plays, the faster his lips vibrate and for Louis, a high note specialist who played for hours each day, the strain on his lips must have been incredible. He blew out a chunk of his upper lip and the resulting scar was prominently visible for the rest of his life. But Louis's recordings in Paris in October 1934 show him in fine form, and it's possible that Louis feigned lip trouble — one of the only plausible excuses under his control — to slip out of Canetti's grasp. Whatever the situation, Canetti cancelled Louis's remaining engagements and then sued Louis for breach of contract.

In January 1935, Louis returned to New York. Just as when he had arrived in Europe two and a half years earlier, he was switching continents to escape a massive managerial mess. He would finally find the manager he so desperately needed in Joe Glaser.

ABOVE A dapper young Armstrong poses by a Métro entrance in Montparnasse. (Paris, 1934)

LEFT Scrapbook number 6 in the Armstrong Archives is filled with clippings from Louis's 1932 tour of England.

RIGHT Louis's hand-decorated tape box shows a smiling Louis and Glaser, side by side.

OPPOSITE PAGE Louis and Joe Glaser. (1965) (Photo by John Loengard)

LOUIS AND JOE GLASER

Perhaps the most influential relationship in Louis's life, outside of those with his wives, was his relationship with Joe Glaser. Glaser was a fascinating, Runyonesque character who by his own design grew to become one of the most powerful figures in the booking of black entertainment. A biography of Joe Glaser is long overdue in jazz literature but its creation is hindered by the fact that Glaser was intensely private about his business affairs, shunned interviews, and derived part of his power from remaining discreetly behind the scenes.

He was born in Chicago circa 1897 to a prominent physician and his wife. After attempting medical school and then used-car sales, he began to manage saloons, and by the mid-1920s he had become the manager of the Sunset Café, one of the most popular black and tan clubs on Chicago's South Side. It was at the Sunset Café that he first met Louis when Louis was performing there with Carroll Dickerson in 1926.

Soon after Louis's return to the United States in 1935, he looked up Joe Glaser. Louis remembered that Glaser had been helpful to him at the Sunset Café and he probably sensed that Glaser had the personality and the connections to rescue him from his entanglements. Glaser and Louis entered into a handshake agreement that lasted for the rest of their lives. After Louis came under Glaser's management, his long-simmering problems with Tommy Rockwell, Johnny Collins, and N.J. Canetti evaporated. Glaser joined the Rockwell-O'Keefe Agency (Tommy Rockwell's firm) with Louis as his sole client.

During the next three decades, Glaser and Louis made each other rich and famous. Glaser moved to New York and founded the Associated Booking Corporation. With Louis as a bargaining chip, Glaser could increase the bookings for his other clients. ("You can have Louis in your club that week if you have Charlie Shavers in your club the following week.") Associated Booking eventually built a client

roster that, over the years, included — in addition to Louis — Duke Ellington, Benny Goodman, Lionel Hampton, Billie Holiday, Ella Fitzgerald, Woody Herman, Cab Calloway, Dinah Washington, Sammy Kaye, Les Brown, Pearl Bailey, Peggy Lee, Stan Kenton, Dave Brubeck, the Kingston Trio, Barbra Streisand, the Rascals, and Creedence Clearwater Revival. Louis made best-selling recordings, appeared in feature films, was a guest on all of the top radio and television shows, was a spokesperson in television ads, appeared in magazine endorsements, and toured all over the world to sold out crowds. They enjoyed a beautiful, weird, symbiotic relationship. Glaser took care of the business end — marketing, bookings, itineraries, payroll, taxes, royalties, residuals, etc. — all Louis had to do was to walk out on stage and play.

Glaser relished a well-deserved reputation for being a shrewd businessman and a hard-nosed negotiator. He was once quoted as saying, "You don't know me, but you know two things about me. I have a terrible temper and I always keep my word."[34] Glaser maintained an old fashioned way of doing business — his word was better than a dozen attorney-reviewed, notary-verified contracts.

LEFT This unsigned watercolor is reminiscent of the advice that Slippers (the nightclub bouncer) gave to Louis just before he left New Orleans to join King Oliver.

RIGHT Joe Glazer's champion Boston Terrier, Debbie, is featured on the cover of this issue of *Dog World*. It is autographed, "To Satchmo, From Debbie, Joe Glazer."

A 1946 letter that Glaser wrote to Joe Garland, the musical director and straw boss for the Louis Armstrong Orchestra, reveals Glaser's intelligence and toughness, and his temper. It also documents the demise of the big band era. The Armstrong Orchestra wore uniforms and each musician had five dollars per week deducted from his salary to pay for his uniforms. Apparently Garland had written to Glaser complaining that Frenchy, the road manager who operated under Glaser's direction, had increased each man's payment from five dollars to ten dollars. Glaser dictated a one and one-third page letter, parts of which read:

> First of all, I want you to know I never knew of any agreement having been made whereby the men would only pay back $5 a week and I cannot understand who made it or why because there is no band in the business that is able to get uniforms at $70 a piece and pay back only $5 per week....

> The boys should be ashamed of complaining - as far as work is concerned they have been working more than any band in the business. I took jobs for them regardless of whether the office received commission or not and even went to extremes to see that they are happy at all times so why they should complain about paying $10 a week back on clothes they have to buy in order to make a living is beyond me so all I can say is I'm sorry but there is nothing I can do in the matter - I definitely insist that Frenchy get back $10 a week on the uniforms and I assure you I will not get involved in matters of this kind again.

> ...Promoters all over are going broke - bookings are being cancelled at the last minute - I can name at least half a dozen Colored bands that will disband in the next 30 days and at least 20 white bands that will disband so if our men are complaining then all I can say is God bless them all and my only hope is that they change before it is too late as I assure you they will be very unhappy unless the situation changes in the immediate future.[35]

Glaser wasn't kidding. Within twelve months of writing this letter, he disbanded the Louis Armstrong Orchestra.

When explaining his relationship with Glaser, Louis often recounted advice that he had been given to him as a young man in New Orleans. He had just received the telegram from Joe Oliver inviting him to move to Chicago and join the Creole Jazz Band. Knowing that Louis had never left New Orleans except for some riverboat excursions, a tough, street-wise nightclub bouncer named Slippers[36] imparted some advice:

> When you go up north, Dipper [Louis's nickname], be sure and get yourself a white man that will put his hand on your shoulder and say "This is my nigger." Those were his exact words... And he was right...because the white man was Joe Glaser."[37]

In Glaser, Louis discovered a powerful protector who was totally devoted to his client. He would never have to worry about gangsters with revolvers, crooked nightclub owners, and underreported record sales again. But the subservience inherent in Slipper's advice was no doubt a component of Glaser and Louis's complicated relationship. Louis almost always referred to his manager, even in casual conversation, as "Mr. Glaser." A 1965 photo by John Loengard captures a telling moment in which a sharply dressed Glaser is speaking to Louis, who, dressed in band uniform, stares at the floor. And a framed, unsigned watercolor discovered in the Armstrong House, recreates Slipper's advice — perhaps unknowingly — by depicting a grinning, hunched over Louis with Joe Glaser's hand on his shoulder.[38]

Some musicians of the Glaser era believed that Glaser cared much more about making money than about Louis's well being and that, in Glaser's eyes, Louis was merely the golden goose. But Glaser and Louis truly loved and respected each other. In 2000-2001 the Louis Armstrong Archives mounted an exhibit about Louis Armstrong and Joe Glaser. To select materials to display, I combed the Archives to find every mention of Glaser. Surely, in the dozens of hours of candidly recorded, dressing-room conversations or in the unpublished manuscripts I would find an off-hand criticism of Glaser. I didn't. Even when hanging out with musician buddies, swapping dirty jokes and carrying on, Louis always spoke of Glaser with respect and sincere affection.

The essential trade off between Louis and Glaser was that Louis would perform, record, or appear wherever Glaser told him to, and then in turn Louis would have whatever he wanted. Louis was content with his house in Queens and keeping Lucille attired in furs and jewelry. Whatever Louis and Lucille wanted, Glaser would take care of it. But Louis was famously generous to others. Reportedly, Louis would ask Glaser to buy a car for a friend down on his luck, Glaser would hit the roof, and then he would purchase the car. Louis would ask Glaser to wire someone money, Glaser would complain, and then he would wire the money. Phoebe Jacobs, who worked for Associated Booking, recalled that Louis once asked the office to ship a new refrigerator to his sister in New Orleans, and within a day Phoebe took care of it. She remembers that Louis typically held court in the dressing room with a roll of bills in the right pocket of his jacket for him, and a roll of bills in the left pocket for surreptitious handouts to others. Glaser instructed Phoebe — who would run errands at the bank for Louis — to reduce the denominations of the bills from fifties to twenties so that hopefully Louis would give away less money.

Today, there exist few primary sources to document the decades-long financial relationship between Glaser and Louis. In the Armstrong Archives are a handful of unsigned performance contracts (all from 1969-1971), several royalty statements from ASCAP, Lucille's bank statements, receipts for major purchases, and other household papers. An accurate accounting of the how the money flowed may never be discovered.

OPPOSITE PAGE Pastel of Joe Glaser, Louis's manager from 1935-1969.

One of Glaser's hobbies was raising champion show dogs and his posh penthouse apartment in midtown Manhattan reportedly had a dog run on the terrace. In 1948, his champion Boston Terrier "Yankee Debutant," who was nicknamed "Debbie," won Best in Show at two major dog shows and also received the coveted Charles O'Connor Memorial Trophy. Among the periodicals in the Louis Armstrong Collection is the December 1949 issue of *Dog World*,[39] a special "Christmas Issue," that has on its cover a photograph of an alert looking Yankee Debutant. The cover is autographed, in Glaser's hand, to read, "To Satchmo from Debbie & Joe Glaser." Glaser gave Louis a feisty Boston Terrier named General and the Armstrong Archives has several wonderful photos of Louis with General, including a series of photos of Louis making General leap to retrieve potato chips from his outstretched hand. And in one of those wonderfully serendipitous intersections of archival materials, the Armstrong Archives also has a reel-to-reel tape that Louis recorded of — guess what? — Louis making General leap to retrieve potato chips. The Boston Terrier's growl overloads the tape deck's little microphone. Years later Glaser arranged for Louis and Lucille to have a pair of Schnauzers:

> We have two dogs. They are Schnauzers, Male + Female. And they are two very fine watch dogs. They not only Bark when the door bell rings, but anybody who Comes' up our steps' they Bark their (A)spirin off. The Male Dog who is the older one' his name is TRUMPET. The Female, the baby' her name is TRINKET — I gave Trumpet to Lucille and Mr. Joe Glaser gave us Trinket. And when the two of them start barking together — Oh Boy what a Duet.[40]

In 1969 Glaser suffered a massive stroke and was raced to Beth Israel Hospital. Coincidentally, Louis was at the same time a patient in Beth Israel for heart and kidney ailments. The hospital staff was instructed to hide the news from Louis that Glaser had been admitted but someone let it slip. Louis made his way to Glaser's room and — to his shock — saw him in a coma. Louis had just begun, while in the hospital, to write a detailed account of his childhood in New Orleans. He turned to a fresh page and in an unsteady hand wrote:

> I dedicate this book
> to my manager and pal
> Mr. Joe Glaser
> the best Friend
> that I've ever had
> May the Lord Bless Him
> Watch over him always.
> His boy + disciple who loved him dearly.
> Louis
>   Satchmo
>   Armstrong[41]

Glaser passed away five weeks later without regaining consciousness.

LOUIS AND MARIJUANA

When I give presentations to high schools, during the concluding question and answer session a student will sometimes ask, "Did Louis use drugs?" And I provide an honest answer. Yes, it is well known by Armstrong aficionados that Louis was a frequent pot smoker. But, Louis was also one of the great geniuses of western music, a tireless workhorse who maintained a demanding schedule of concerts, recording sessions, and travel, and a consummate professional who was always on time and ready to perform. That Louis smoked pot does not prove the inverse: Smoking pot doesn't make you a musical genius, a tireless worker, and a consummate professional.

An uninhibited moment in the Braddock Hotel. Note the silly grins, the air freshening atomizer, and the marijuana cigarettes in the hands in the right side of the photo. (1940s) (Photo by Charles Peterson)

Does the Armstrong Archives contain evidence of Louis's marijuana smoking? We certainly didn't find his stash, or rolling papers, or any other paraphernalia. (People ask me if we did.) Louis had passed away twenty years before we began to process the collection and any materials that may have been in the house at his death had long since disappeared. But the collections do contain some documentation, all of it interesting. A photo taken by Charles Peterson in the Braddock Hotel in 1942 shows Louis and several friends. They are obviously stoned — lowered eyelids and sly smiles for the entire group is the giveaway — and the presence of an air freshening atomizer, humorously demonstrated by Louis, is tantalizingly suspicious. But look closely at the right hand that appears in the far right of the photo — the hand's owner is out of the camera's view — and the right hand of the young lady standing next to Louis. Sure enough, each of the hands is pinching between thumb and forefinger a "roach," i.e., the nub of an almost finished marijuana cigarette.

Circa 1955, many jazz musicians received and were requested to anonymously complete a two-page, twelve-question survey about drug use in the jazz world. The survey was supposedly the project of a magazine which was considering writing an article on drug use amongst jazz musicians — but jazz experts whom I have asked about the survey cannot verify this. (In the post Charlie Parker years, drug use among jazz musicians was a compelling topic, although statistically, more medical doctors than jazz musicians were addicted to heroin.) The Archives acquired a photocopy of Louis's completed questionnaire in 1997. His answers are non sequiturs, but, as was so typical of Louis, he provided beautiful answers to stupid questions.

1) At what percent do you place the users of narcotics in the Jazz field?

> *The music that comes out of a man's horn is good enough for me — his personal habit*
> *I don't care.*

2) Of the above, what do you believe is the percentage of addicts?

> *In the days when I came up with the old greats in New Orleans — we didn't have*
> *time to worry about little stupid things—his ability was good enough for us.*

His answer to Question Nine indicates that Louis considered the enjoyment of marijuana to be completely divorced from the use of "dope or narcotics," i.e., heroin.

9) Do you believe that the percentage of users among Negro musicians is higher than among White musicians? A) Yes. B) No.

> *To tell you the truth — I have never witnessed anyone using 'dope or 'Norcotics" in my life.*

In 1998, *High Times* magazine did a feature story on Louis and the issue's centerfold displayed a golden cornet that had a bell overflowing filled with buds.[42] A few months later, *High Times* posthumously inducted Louis into its Counterculture Hall of Fame. Inductees are presented with the Cannabis Cup award. High Times graciously invited to fly me to Amsterdam during their annual "growers convention" to accept the award, but, for obvious reasons, I declined. Armstrong friend Jack Bradley (whom you'll read more about later), traveled to Amsterdam and accepted the little gold plated trophy, shaped like a loving cup with marijuana leaves growing up the sides. Upon his return to the United States, he donated it to the Archives.

RIGHT Louis and Alpha. (Early 1930s)

BELOW The hand writing on the back of this snapshot reads, "Just leaving Nottingham, Eng., August 1932."

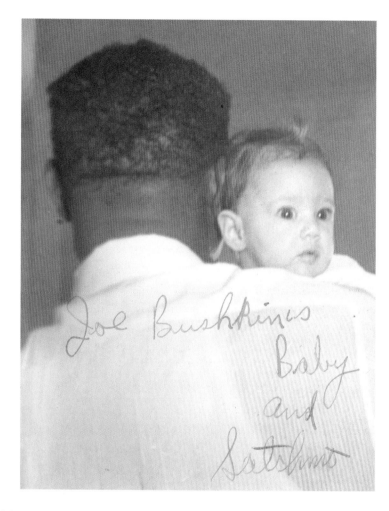

RIGHT "Joe Buskin's Baby and Satchmo." This is Nina Buskin Lerner, the daughter of pianist Joe Bushkin.

OPPOSITE PAGE LEFT John Newmann met Louis on three occasions. Celebrating his eleventh birthday, he sat in with the All Stars at the Blue Note.

OPPOSITE PAGE RIGHT Two years later, Newmann again sat in at the Blue Note.

LOUIS AND KIDS

Although Louis never fathered any children of his own[43] — and he was married four times — Louis loved kids. That Louis loved kids and kids loved Louis is no surprise. All artistic creativity is rooted in playfulness and Louis was a child at heart.

The Armstrong Archives overflows with evidence that children were a major source of joy to Louis. There are dozens of photographs of Louis and children together, including dressing room photos of fans who have come backstage to greet Louis and get an autograph and snapshots of Louis with kids in the neighborhood. When documentary photographer John Loengard spent a summer day with Louis in 1965 for an article that would appear in Life magazine, he took some spectacular photos of Louis with kids from the community. (The photos were not used in the article but Loengard gave professional prints to Louis.) In one photo, taken in Louis's backyard at 8:50 p.m. (look closely at Louis's watch), Louis has pushed aside a plate of chicken and rice to sign an autograph for a young boy. Just behind them stand two other slightly older boys who are studying the autograph that they just got. And in the background are several other kids, one of whom is looks directly at the camera. A second photo, taken earlier in the day, shows Louis on 107th Street, just a few doors north of his house, carrying on with a group of eight giggling girls. Penciled notes on the back of the photo indicate that the girls loved to hear Louis sing "Hello Dolly" — it had been a huge hit the year before — and that they would stop him on the street and plead, "Sing, 'Dolly'."

Three photos donated to the Archives by Armstrong fan John Newmann document a delightful story. In 1952 John's father took him for his eleventh birthday to the Blue Note in Chicago to hear Louis Armstrong. John had been studying piano, had picked up a little boogie-woogie, and — because he had seen Armstrong on TV and had heard some of his records — was a big Armstrong fan. John's Dad — much to John's embarrassment — proudly announced to Louis that it was his son's birthday and asked John if he was going to tell Louis about his piano playing. Louis — to everybody's shock — invited John to sit in with the band. Sure enough, at the end of the second set, John replaced Earl "Fatha" Hines on piano and delivered two rousing choruses of boogie woogie. A photo taken afterwards in the dressing room shows a delighted, freckle-faced kid with Louis's arm comfortably wrapped around him. Louis autographed the photo "Best wishes to little Johnny from Louis Armstrong." Two years later, a more mature John Newmann — teenage boys grow fast — returned on his thirteenth birthday to see Louis during a matinee appearance at the Blue Note. Upon spotting him during intermission Louis remembered him and asked, "What are you going to play for us today?" John sat in again — this time replacing Billy Kyle — and performed "Stompin' at the Savoy." They had a photo taken (check out John's jazzy shirt with the musical clefs and song titles) and Louis signed it, "Here's Satching atcha." Time marches on. About five years later John is the owner and director of a boys summer day camp. Louis is in town for a week performing at the Tenthouse Theatre. John (we already know he's not shy) approaches Louis and invites him to come to the camp and visit the boys during one of his days in Chicago. Louis's performances are at night he is heavily scheduled during the day, but he promises to come. The word gets out and parents telephone John to ask if they can come to see Louis; John tells all of them, "No, it's just for the campers." Louis shows up one morning in Bermuda shorts and a Hawaiian shirt. He has a ball, particularly when he hears the scat ending that John taught the campers to use when they sang the camp song for Louis. The group photo shows a gaggle of smiling, crew cut kids in t-shirts posing with a jubilant Armstrong. A fulfilled John Newmann — who has now grown into a lanky teenager — stands to the right of Louis in the back row.

When John was a summer camp counselor, Louis — while in town for a week-long engagement — stopped by to visit the kids. Newmann is second from left in the back row. (Photos courtesy of John Newman.)

[1] Louis Armstrong. *Satchmo: My Life in New Orleans* (New York: Prentice Hall, 1954. Reprint: New York: Da Capo, 1986): 150.

[2] Ibid: 150-151.

[3] Ibid.

[4] Louis Armstrong. "The Armstrong Story." Manuscript 1/1, Louis Armstrong Collection, Louis Armstrong Archives, Queens College.

[5] A famous Chicago dance hall which could hold one thousand patrons. The King Oliver Band was in residence there from 1922 to 1924.

[6] Louis Armstrong, "The Armstrong Story."

[7] Louis Armstrong. "The Goffin Notebooks," Manuscript held by the Institute of Jazz Studies. Published in Louis Armstrong: In His Own Words (New York: Oxford University Press, 1999): 97.

[8] Louis Armstrong, letter to Leonard Feather, October 1, 1941. Photocopy. Satchmo Collection. Louis Armstrong Archives. It has been published in The Louis Armstrong Companion: Eight Decades of Commentary, ed. Joshua Berrett (New York: Schirmer, 1999): 107-122.

[9] Gary Giddins, Satchmo: 92.

[10] Ernie Anderson, "Joe Glaser & Louis Armstrong," Storyville 160 (1 December 1994): 135.

[11] He didn't record "Someday" until 1947.

[12] Louis Armstrong, "Someday You'll Be Sorry." Transcribed from bonus track on reissue of Ambassador Satch (Sony: CK 64926, 2000).

[13] Louis Armstrong, "Why I Like Dark Women," Ebony 9, no. 10 (Aug. 1954): [61-68.]

[14] Louis Armstrong, Untitled manuscript, Manuscript 1/4, Louis Armstrong Collection, Louis Armstrong Archives.

[15] Ibid.

[16] Ibid.

[17] Ibid.

[18] Louis Armstrong. *Satchmo: My Life in New Orleans*: 83.

[19] Ibid: 162.

[20] Ibid: 162.

[21] Louis Armstrong, *"The Goffin Notebooks,"* in Louis Armstrong: In His Own Words: 97.

[22] Ibid: 97-98.

[23] To the best of my knowledge, these photographs were first published in Hugues Panassie, *Louis Armstrong* (New York: Charles Scribner's Sons, 1971) and were made available to Panassie by Jack Bradley.

[24] I was told in 1991 by a member of the Armstrong Foundation that Clarence was dead.

[25] In 1933 Connie's Inn relocated to West 48th Street.

[26] Louis Armstrong, "The Goffin Notebooks": 110

[27] Ibid.

[28] U.S. District Court, Southern District of New York, "Louis Armstrong, plaintiff against Thomas G. Rockwell, Joseph Weber, et al," Photocopy of court docket, Papers 1996-50, Satchmo Collection, Louis Armstrong Archives.

[29] Ibid.

[30] Ibid.

[31] Hugues Pannasié, "Louis Armstrong at the Salle Pleyel (1946)," from Douze Années de Jazz, translated and reprinted in Joshua Berrett, The Louis Armstrong Companion: 63.

[32] Louis Armstrong, Reel 2, Tape Series, Louis Armstrong Collection, Louis Armstrong Archives.

[33] "N. J. Canetti présente Louis Armstrong," Concert Program 1994-8, Satchmo Collection, Louis Armstrong Archives.

[34] "Joe Glaser is Dead at 72," Obituary, New York Times, June 8, 1969.

[35] Joe Glaser, Letter to Joe Garland, 25 July 1946. Phoebe Jacobs Collection, Louis Armstrong Archives.

[36] Louis told and retold this story his entire life. In some accounts the advice came from Slippers and in other accounts it came from Black Benny. Both were older, street-wise men who were attempting to impart their wisdom to young Louis. Both men are mentioned in Satchmo: My Life in New Orleans.

[37] From a letter written by Louis Armstrong. Reprinted in Max Jones and John Chilton, The Louis Armstrong Story, 1900-1971 (London: November Books, 1971, reprint ed., New York: Da Capo, 1988): 17.

[38] After we reproduced this painting on an invitation to our exhibit, "Louis Armstrong and Joe Glaser," we received a letter from a patron complaining that the painting presented an offensive stereotype. In our apology to her we explained that the stereotypical presentation was one of the reasons that the painting was in the exhibit — let's discuss the imagery rather than suppress it — and reminded her that the painting was owned by Louis himself.

[39] *Dog World* 34, no. 12 (December 1949). Periodical 1/2, Louis Armstrong Collection, Louis Armstrong Archives.

[40] Louis Armstrong, "Our Neighborhood," Manuscript 1/11, Louis Armstrong Collection, Louis Armstrong Archives.

[41] Louis Armstrong, "Louis Armstrong — the Jewish Family...," Manuscript 2/5, Louis Armstrong Collection, Louis Armstrong Archives.

[42] *High Times*, 279 (November 1998): 54-64, Periodical 1998-436, Satchmo Collection, Louis Armstrong Archives.

[43] A letter from Louis to Joe Glaser (dated August 2, 1955) reveals that Louis believed that in 1954 or 1955 he fathered a daughter with a mistress but the current view by Armstrong experts is that he is not the father. The letter is owned by the Music Division of the Library of Congress and photocopies of it are held by the Louis Armstrong Archives. It has been published in Louis Armstrong: In His Own Words: 157-163.

Observations from the Front: Twelve Years in the Louis Armstrong House & Archives

In my decade of meeting visitors to the Louis Armstrong House & Archives, presenting public programs about Louis, interviewing his band members, interviewing his neighbors, collecting stories from those who met Louis backstage, and encountering jazz buffs in just about every imaginable situation, I have never heard a bad word about Louis. Never. There is no one else whom I can say that about.

Through a subtle process that still mystifies me, even those with only a hazy understanding of Louis Armstrong exhibit real affection for him. Repairmen, deliverymen, sanitation workers, meter readers, pest control inspectors, and all of the others who arrive at the Armstrong House on business rather than as tourists, no matter what their age or national origin, are slightly in awe of Louis. "You mean, this is where he really lived?" is a typical response. And outside the workplace, when I meet people socially and they eventually find out what I do for a living, the characteristic reaction to hearing the name "Louis Armstrong" is an involuntarily grin.

Louis profoundly touched almost everyone with whom he came into contact. A lady who dropped by the Armstrong Archives one fall morning related to me that in the 1950s she was trapped in a troubled marriage and lived in an isolated region of New England. Not having anyone else to turn to, she poured out her heart in a letter to Louis Armstrong. Even today the woman admits it was an odd, almost inexplicable remedy. Louis answered her letter with sage advice that brought her great comfort. A decade later, she was living in California and was able to talk her way backstage after a Louis Armstrong performance. She mentioned who she was, and to her tearful surprise, Louis perfectly remembered her and her situation and inquired about her welfare with heartfelt sincerity. Today, the letter from Louis is one of this lady's most prized possessions.

Perhaps every celebrity musician has had zealous fans. Frank Sinatra had the screaming bobby-soxers, the Beatles attracted hordes of tearful teenage girls, and even mid-nineteenth century pianist and composer Louis Marie Gottschalk presented "monster concerts" to thousands of adoring fans. But Louis was no mere matinee idol. He touched people in profound ways. Cathan Shoniker of Ontario, Canada, is one such person. She became captivated by Louis's music while a teenager, and for the rest of Louis's life she attended every Louis Armstrong concert within a hundred miles of her home. They became friends of a sort and she recalls that, "His thoughtfulness, and his kindness were unbelievable." Ms. Shoniker told me the following story when we first met. She later included it in a letter:

We invited Louis for dinner one night while he was playing at the Okeefe Centre in downtown Toronto. We lived about 20 miles north in the small town of Aurora. He accepted, and we planned the dinner for Thursday evening. A few days later, my husband and I were sitting with Louis in his dressing room before a performance, when the mayor of Toronto came in and invited Louis to a dinner that the town council was planning as a tribute to him (for that same Thursday). There was a reporter in the room with us, who had been with Louis for a few days doing an in depth story of some kind. Needless to say, I was devastated. My heart sank. Louis never hesitated for a moment. He told the Mayor (and I will never forget his incredible answer), "You should have asked me sooner. I'm going to dinner with friends." This was the mayor of Toronto, a city of three million people. The reporter came over to me and asked, "Are you from New York?" I said "No." "Who are you?" "No one," I said. The reporter just smiled. Louis thanked the stunned mayor for the kind invitation, and never mentioned it again.[1]

Louis truly loved his fans. The website for the Louis Armstrong House & Archives (www.satchmo.net) includes two discussion boards. One of the boards is called "Memories of Louis" and on it we ask visitors who met Louis to share their experiences. Gary Soon recalled that:

Louis and Tyree Glenn in concert. There are only two faces in the crowd that are not smiling. (Photo: John Loengard/Getty Images)

In the early 60's, when Louis Armstrong was performing at The Cave supper club in Vancouver, he asked the club owner where was the best place for Chinese food. The owner was a friend of my late father and asked if he would take Louis out for dinner. I was 11 or 12 at the time, my mom and dad, brother and sister had dinner with Louis, his wife Lucille and his band at a restaurant in Vancouver. After dinner Louis and his wife came over to our home for tea and dessert. We watched the Ed Sullivan Show on TV and Ed announced that Louis was to perform next week. He toured Vancouver several more times at The Cave, and he would have dinner with my family each time he was in town.[2]

Photographer and jazz memorabilia collector Jack Bradley had the great privilege to befriend Louis and to spend much time in his company. Jack was an Armstrong devotee even before they met and the concept of becoming dear friends with him was beyond his imagination. He first spoke to Louis in the early 1950s when he got an autograph after a performance in Hyannis, Massachusetts, near Jack's hometown. But after Jack moved to New York City in 1958, he met Louis through their mutual friend Jeann Failows. Louis invited Jack to visit him in his Corona home. The big day arrived. Jack entered Louis's den and the two men greeted each other. But soon Jack, overwhelmed with the realization that he was standing next to his hero, became speechless. On the verge of weeping, Jack eventually blurted out, "I'm awfully sorry, I just don't know what to say." Louis reached around him and patted him on the shoulder, saying comfortingly, "That's all right, Pops — everything's cool." Today Jack still chokes up when he remembers Louis's gentle affection.

Jack is a collector's collector. He and his wife Nancy live in a little house on Cape Cod stuffed to the rafters with jazz memorabilia. (Nancy's rule for many years has been that the kitchen, bathroom, and dining room are off limits to collectibles; and sure enough, every remaining space is packed with Jack's treasures.) Among his many Armstrong wonders are a brick and a piece of the banister from the Colored Waif's Home for Boys; rare movie posters and lobby cards for motion pictures in which Louis appeared; a stunning compilation of 16 mm prints of Louis in motion pictures, television shows, and television commercials; Armstrong dolls and figurines; thousands of photos; hundreds of books and periodicals; and a nearly comprehensive collection of Armstrong LPs and 78s. Louis, knowing Jack's love for him and his passion for collecting, gave Jack many items over the years. Jack has Louis's own clothes that Louis gave him, including two wool sport coats and a pair of leather slippers. He owns a pair of wire rim eyeglasses that Louis discarded after the doctor changed Louis's prescription. Decades later, Jack being the collector that he is, took the lenses to an optometrist to determine what the prescription is, so that he could note it for historians. One day, while Jack was visiting Louis in his den, Louis opened a desk drawer filled with publicity photos and, knowing Jack's affection for such things, suggested that he pick out some photos to keep. Jack selected six photos, and then Louis offered to autograph one of them. He chuckled and wrote, "To Jack Bradley, The 'Greatest' Photo Taker, Your Boy Satch, Louis Armstrong." Jack, who at this time was serving as Louis's official photographer, thanked him profusely but inwardly he was embarrassed. He inferred that Louis, whom he knew had had only a few years of formal schooling, was obviously intimidated by the word "photographer" and had instead written "Photo Taker." Only decades later did Jack suddenly get the joke: "Photo Taker" referred to his predilection for carrying home photographs, as well as eyeglasses, clothing, correspondence, and other relics of his hero's life. Louis, not one to spoil a good joke, had never explained the pun.

What did Louis see in Jack Bradley that cemented this somewhat unusual friendship? The two men were thirty years apart in age. One was an international celebrity, a jazz musician born in New Orleans. And the other was a passionate jazz listener, a merchant marine and amateur photographer from Cape Cod. Louis knew that Jack loved him and just wanted to be around him. Sure, Jack was a collector, but his collecting derived from his worship of Louis. He didn't collect primarily to resell items on the market (which he could have easily done) and to make money (which he surely could have used); he collected chiefly because his acquisitions reminded him of Louis. He collected for remembrance of his beloved. Almost everyone who hung around Louis wanted something for themselves: the thrill of being associated with a celebrity, an autographed photo to show their co-workers, a twenty-dollar handout, a story for their newspaper, a chance for Louis to record the song they were writing, etc. But Jack — who recalls that, "at various times I served as his chauffeur, cook, connection and photographer — Most of all, I was his friend"[3] — simply wanted to be near Louis. And Louis understood that.

I haven't yet succumbed to the temptation to deify Louis. He was as human as the rest of us, and was certainly no saint. But I do subscribe to the notion that, as is possible with any artistic genius, he drew heavily from a higher power. Genius by itself is no guarantee that an artist shall also have a positive impact on the mundane world around him; witness the troubled everyday lives of Beethoven, Charlie Parker, Billie Holiday, and a host of others. But Louis seemed to embody love, goodness, and humility in everything he touched.

Louis had a temper, but it seemed to be directed more at injustices than at personal frustration with things not going his way. Louis's response to the 1957 Little Rock crisis is a good example.[4] After watching a television news broadcast showing an angry mob spitting upon black school children, an outraged Louis told a reporter that Arkansas Governor Orville Faubus was "an uneducated plowboy," and that President Eisenhower—who had not yet made any attempt to intervene and defuse the volatile situation — was "two faced" and "had no guts." Louis was scheduled to tour the Soviet Union — he would have been the first jazz artist to do so — but he abruptly cancelled the tour, complaining that, "The way they're treating my people in the south the government can go to Hell," and "How can I represent my country when they are treating my people that way." Yes, Louis was angry, but his outrage was directly at a profound social injustice.

Louis's tapes capture numerous moments when Louis could be expected to be outraged, but isn't. He relates a fair number of stories of racial discrimination in his past, but his attitude is often one of pity for the discriminators and the accounts are delivered in a "Can you believe this one?" mode of story-telling. One such tape has as its participants Louis Armstrong, Doc Pugh (Louis's long-time valet), and saxophonist Eddie "Clean Head" Vinson. The topic being discussed is how white people can say hurtful things to black people, without even realizing what they are doing. Louis provides an example:

> If we wasn't recording, I'd put on that reel that I made in Honolulu with the boy that was driving us...and it will verify it. Now, after we've come off the bandstand, we had a little dressing room up there. And wasn't nobody up there.. Pugh will tell you about it. And this boy that drives. After the dance. Everybody's gone. So this white boy, he's about 23 or 25, I'd say. And he's from Texas. He said, "Well, Louie Armstrong, I want to shake your hand." See? "And I'm

going to be very frank with you." See? "I don't like Negroes." See what I mean? I say, "Well, damn, you're pretty frank about it." You know? "My family taught me to hate Negroes." He's from some little town. And after we finished, I'm going to put this on, you know?...He said, "But you, I like you." So, by this time Gary is getting ready to grab that motherfucker's throat...He said, "You go through this little old town," whatever the name is, and he said, "You look my brother up, cause he's one of your fans." See? So now Gary's done got him over in the corner... "I just don't like niggers, but I like him!" You know? You can't get away from that. So that makes it true. There's always some white man that likes one nigger at least![5]

To state that Louis was patient or forgiving or tolerant — as some observers have — misses the point. Patience and forgiveness and tolerance — although admirable — still imply the condescension of someone who has been unjustly wronged. Louis often times seemed to function from a higher, more compassionate plane in which wrong or right is irrelevant.

Louis sometimes had a profoundly positive impact on the troubled world around him. During his second tour of Africa, in 1960, when he departed the Congo River ferry, the opposing forces of Joseph Mobutu and Patrice Lumumba, who were engaged in a bitter civil war, halted their fighting and jointly escorted him to the stadium. Arvell Shaw (who played bass for Louis for more than twenty-five years) recalled that while performing a weeklong engagement in East Berlin, the band members discovered that, after their show, the only recreation available to them was to retire to a dingy hotel and have a bowl of soup. By the third night, desperate for entertainment, they decided to cross over to West Berlin to explore the nightlife. When they arrived at the East German checkpoint, they were surrounded by soldiers armed with machine guns who demanded a pass that the band did not have. But once the soldiers aimed their flashlights into the bus, they shouted "Louis Armstrong! Louis Armstrong!" and waved the bus on. When the bus arrived at Checkpoint Charlie, the American soldiers were astonished that a vehicle had crossed over without a pass. Then they spotted its famous passenger, cried "Satchmo!" and allowed the bus to go through. The band repeated this routine for each night of their stay in Berlin.[6]

I sometimes envision Louis's achievements as facets of a diamond. His trumpet playing, singing, composing, acting, collage making, letter writing, tape recording, philanthropy, and genuine care and concern for other people are all differently angled views of the same sparkling gem. What especially interests me is the light that flows through this diamond and makes it sparkle. Perhaps the source of that light is indicated in a letter that Louis wrote to Max Jones. Writing in the twilight of his life — a life that included incredible childhood poverty, months in a reform school, corrupt managers, racial discrimination, and the burdens of celebrity, but a life that also included wealth, fame, the love of friends and family, the adoration of fans, and most of all, the transcendence of art — Louis declared that:

Now I must tell you that my whole life has been happiness. Through all of the misfortunes, etc. I did not plan anything. Life was there for me and I accepted it. And life, what ever came out, has been beautiful to me, and I love everybody.[7]

[1] Letter from Cathan Shoniker to Michael Cogswell, 30 July 2001. Vertical file, Louis Armstrong Archives.

[2] Gary Soon, posting to www.satchmo.net, March 5, 2002

[3] Jack Bradley, unpublished essay, c. 1970s, Louis Armstrong Archives.

[4] Perhaps the most complete account of Louis and Little Rock crisis is in: Michael Meckna, "Louis Armstrong Blasts Little Rock, Arkansas," Perspectives on American Music since 1950, ed. James R. Heintze (New York: Garland, 1999): 141-151.

[5] Reel 115, Louis Armstrong Collection, Louis Armstrong Archives.

[6] Oral History interview with Arvell Shaw, March 21, 1995, Satchmo Collection, Louis Armstrong Archives

[7] Louis Armstrong, Letter to Max Jones, reprinted in Jones and Chilton, Louis: 15.

ABOVE Everybody has a good time when Louis is around. How could they not?

LEFT Louis's joy is contagious. Radio broadcast, 1940s.

Acknowledgments

If I were to thank all of the people who contributed to the establishment of the Louis Armstrong House & Archives, all of the people who support our programs and services, and all of the people who assisted with the creation of this book, my thank you list would fill another volume. I have attempted to thank as many as practical, and if I left you out, please accept my apologies.

As described in some detail in Chapters II and III, there would not even be a Louis Armstrong House Museum or a Louis Armstrong Archives if it were not for David Gold and Phoebe Jacobs of the Louis Armstrong Educational Foundation. It was their vision that enabled the Armstrong House and its contents to be saved from sale to the highest bidder and preserved by Queens College. And the annual funding provided by the Louis Armstrong Educational Foundation (its trustees and officers are a who's who of the jazz world) is the bedrock of our general operating budget.

There are many at Queens College who assist us in numerous ways. Queens College President James Muyskens has provided vital encouragement and support ever since he first arrived on campus. And without the contributions of Sue Henderson, Ann Cohen, and Jane Denkensohn, this book would never have come to fruition. During the past decade, we have been greatly helped by Shirley Strum Kenny, Stephen Curtis, Allen Lee Sessoms, Russ Hotzler, Susan Zimmerman, Ceil Cleveland, Florence Luckow, Nancy Zemsky, Mike Prasad, Howard Brofsky, Matt Simon, and many, many others.

We have been blessed with an immensely talented staff at the Louis Armstrong House & Archives over the years. Our current crew — Peggy Alexander, Kendal Albert, Baltsar Beckeld, and Matthew Sohn — work extremely hard but never lose their sense of humor. Past employees who deserve special recognition include Bessie Williams, Richard Loyd, and Deslyn Downes.

Louis and Lucille's neighbors, who have been eager to see a museum blossom in their community, have given us invaluable advice and encouragement. Selma Heraldo, next-door neighbor and "Queen of the Block," deserves special recognition as a close personal friend of the Armstrongs who keeps their legacy alive through her good works. Other friends and community leaders include Andrew Jackson, Grace Lawrence, Jimmy Heath (yes, the famous saxophonist), Terry Obradovitch, Jimmy Smith, Giovanna Read, and legendary soul food caterer Minnie Vaughan.

Converting a private home into a historic house museum would not have been possible without the support of elected officials. Queens Borough President Helen Marshall, former Borough President Claire Shulman, City Councilman Hiram Monserrate, State Assemblyman José Peralta, State Assemblyman Jeff Aubrey, U.S. Senator Hillary Clinton, U.S. Representative Joseph Crowley, and other officials have all contributed their precious time and influence to this project.

The Louis Armstrong House is owned by the New York City Department of Cultural Affairs and administered by Queens College under a long-term license agreement. And our annual Pops is Tops children's concerts are underwritten by a programs grant from the Department of Cultural Affairs. Special thanks are due to Commissioner Kate Levin as well as to Susan Chin, Victor Metoyer, Kathy Hughes, Marc Hsaio, and former Commissioner Schuyler Chapin.

The Louis Armstrong House & Archives has long benefited from an active and engaged Advisory Board comprised of community leaders, archives and museum specialists, jazz experts, and development professionals. Many

Advisory Board members are cited elsewhere in these Acknowledgements, but immense thanks are also due to (in alphabetical order) Jerry Chazen, Stanley Crouch, Mario DellaPina, John Fleckner, Mitchell Grubler, Wynton Marsalis, Vicki Match Suna, Dr. Billy Taylor, and George Wein. The programs and services of the Louis Armstrong House & Archives exist only because of the generosity of our funders. In addition to the support of the Louis Armstrong Educational Foundation, we are especially grateful to the National Endowment for the Humanities, Save America's Treasures Program, American Express, KeySpan Foundation, New York Community Trust, John Van Rens and Sarah Lutz, and our steadily growing membership. (Have you become a member?)

The list of architects, engineers, contactors, conservators, consultants, construction managers, and trades people that helped create the museum is far too long to cite. But special mention must be given to Platt Byard Dovell White Architects, Rogers-Marvel Architects, NSP Enterprises, Jablonski-Berkowitz Conservation, Stephen Saitas Designs, and the New York City Department of Design and Construction. I have been privileged to hang out with musicians who performed with Louis. Each of them has enough memories to fill several books. Especially generous with their time have been Joe Muranyi, Marty Napoleon, Joe Bushkin, Ed Swanston, and the late Arvell Shaw.

Literary agent Tony Shugaar realized that there was a book waiting to be written and believed in the book even when he had no justification to. Publisher Richard Perry and designer Wade Daughtry of Collectors Press also immediately recognized what the book should be. Taking 35,000 words of questionable prose and 300 images of Satchmo's stuff, they stirred them and mixed them and seasoned them and baked them to create a feast of a book. Various drafts of the manuscript were reviewed by Dan Morgenstern, Jack Bradley, David Ostwald, and the entire staff of the Louis Armstrong House & Archives. Any mistakes in the text result from my own shortcomings. Dan Morgenstern, who has long been one of my heroes, composed a Foreword that gives me undue praise. He is one of the true giants in the study of jazz history, and anyone who has had the joy of working with him will easily remember his remarkable ability to gently close his eyes, focus within, and tell you each name, date, and location that you inquired about, as well as to explain "what really happened."

Photographer Lisa Kahane has worked with the Louis Armstrong House & Archives since 1991. She has an extraordinary ability to capture the beauty in what, to some eyes, would simply be a tape box plastered with old photos and covered with yellowing Scotch tape. Thanks are also due to those who graciously permitted their photos to be reproduced in this book: Jack Bradley, William Carter, Charles Graham, Lisa Gherkin, and John Newmann.

David Ostwald, as an Advisory Board member, trustee of the Louis Armstrong Educational Foundation, tubist, and Grammy-nominated bandleader (The Gully Low Jazz Band) rivals Louis in generosity. He has selflessly served the Louis Armstrong House & Archives on numerous occasions, including providing pro bono legal services. (He's a tubist first, and a partner in a Manhattan law firm second.)

Armstrong devotees Ostwald, Jack Bradley, and George Avakian have, during the past twelve years, freely provided me immeasurable assistance in countless ways. I am grateful for all that they have done and continue to do, but even more, I cherish their personal friendship. They are true believers in the ability of Louis's life and music to make this world a better place.

Finally, I am eternally indebted to my darling wife, Dale Van Dyke. During our years together, I have been a professional musician, a graduate student, a music archivist, and now a museum director. Dale has responded to late bedtimes, missed meals, evening events, working on weekends, out-of-town trips, sleepless nights, and my infatuation with Louis Armstrong with nothing but love and encouragement. "La Vie en Rose."

MICHAEL COGSWELL
March 2003